Foundation Chemistry

For Class X

Part-2 of 2

NOTION PRESS

NOTION PRESS

India. Singapore. Malaysia.

ISBN xxx-x-xxxxx-xx-x

Dedicated to our Beloved Prime Minister Shree Narendra Modi ji, whose life gives the Inspiration to every Individual

If a Man ***Decides*** *to achieve something in his life nothing is Impossible*

कर्मण्येवाधिकारस्ते मा फलेषु कदाचन।

मा कर्मफलहेतुर्भूर्मा ते सङ्गोऽस्त्वकर्मणि॥ २-४७

Karmanye vadhikaraste Ma Phaleshu Kadachana,

Ma Karmaphalaheturbhurma Te Sangostvakarmani

You have the right to work only but never to its fruits.

Let not the fruits of action be your motive, nor let your attachment be to inaction.

CONTENT

TOPIC NAME	PAGE NO.

4. CARBON & ITS COMPOUNDS

5. PERIODIC CLASSIFICATION

4 CARBON & ITS COMPOUNDS

4.1 INTRODUCTION :

Materials like food, cosmetics, furnitures, clothes, medicines, books and many other things contain the versatile element **carbon**.

In addition, all living creatures (human beings, animals, birds, insects, plant kingdom etc.) are made up of **carbon compounds** (Such as fats, carbohydrates, proteins, vitamins, hormones, etc.)

The amount of carbon present in the earth's crust or in the atmosphere is low.

The earth's crust has **0.02% carbon** in the form of salts, like carbonates, bicarbonates,metallic cyanides, coal, petroleum, graphite etc. Earth's atmosphere has **0.03% of carbon dioxide**.

4.2 BONDING IN CARBON COMPOUND :

We know that the reactivity of elements is explained as their tendency to attain a fulfilled outer shell, that is, to attain a **noble gas electronic configuration**.

Elements forming ionic compounds achieve this by either gaining or losing electrons from the outermost shell.

In the case of carbon, Carbon has 6 protons, 6 neutrons and 6 electrons. Its chemical symbol is ${}^{12}_{6}C$. Its electronic configuration is 2 electrons in the K-shell, and 4 electrons in the L-shell. It has four electrons in its outermost shell and needs to gain or lose four electrons to attain noble gas configuration.

(i) If it gains four electrons forming C^{4-} anion. It would be difficult for the nucleus with six protons to hold on to ten electrons, means attraction force of 6 protons is not sufficient to hold 8 electrons in valence shell.

(ii) If it loses four electrons forming C^{4+} cation. It would require a large amount of energy to remove four electrons from its valence shell that is not easily available in chemical reaction.

So it does not form ionic bond at all, Carbon shares its valence electrons with other atoms of carbon or with atoms of other elements. Not just carbon, but many other elements form molecules by sharing electrons in this manner.

The shared electrons 'belong' to the outer shells of both the atoms and lead to both atoms attaining the noble gas configuration.

➢ **Covalent Bond :**

"A covalent bond, also called **molecular bond**, is a chemical bond that involves the sharing of electron pairs between atoms. These electron pairs are known as shared pairs or bonding pair, and the stable balance of attractive and repulsive forces between atoms, when they share electrons, is known as **covalent bonding**."

For example :

$$H\bullet + *H \longrightarrow H\overset{\bullet}{_*}H \longrightarrow H-H \text{ or } H_2 \text{ molecule.}$$

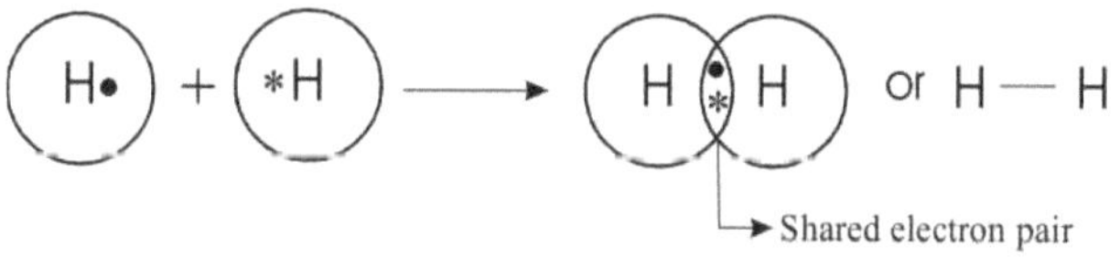

Some simple examples of covalent bonded compounds are:

➤ **Single Covalent Bond:**

When one electron is shared from both atoms a single covalent bond is formed. This bond is indicated by a single line (–) between two bonding atoms.

Formation of chlorine molecule :

At.no. (Z) of Cl = 17 Electronic configuration = K(2) L(8) M(7)

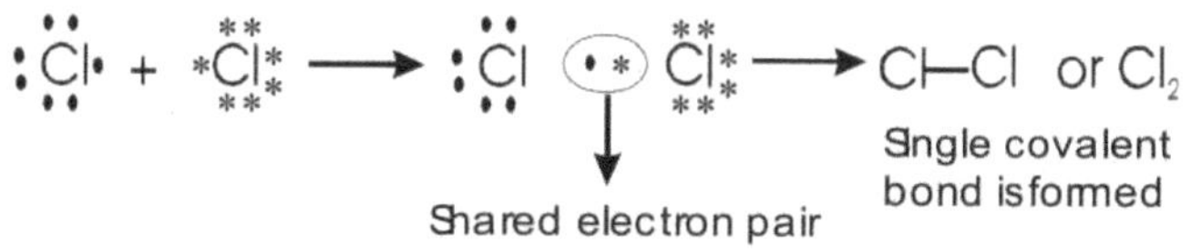

Formation of Ammonia :

At. no. (Z) of N = 7 Electronic configuration of N = K(2) L (5)

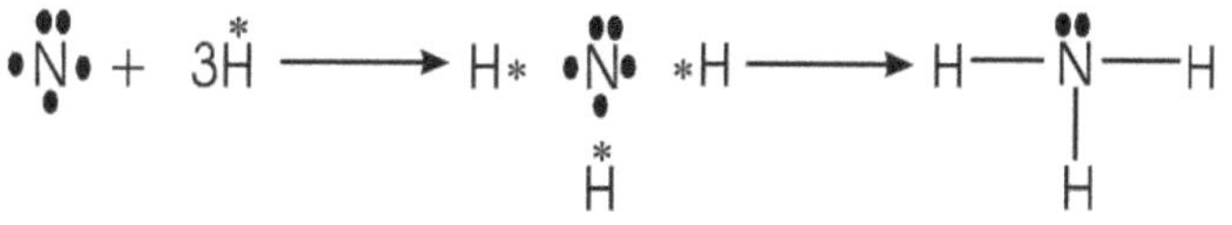

or NH_3 (Three single bond are formed)

Formation of methane (CH_4)

At. no. of C(Z) = 6 At. no. of H(Z) = 1

E.C. of C = K(2) L(4) E.C. of H = K (1)

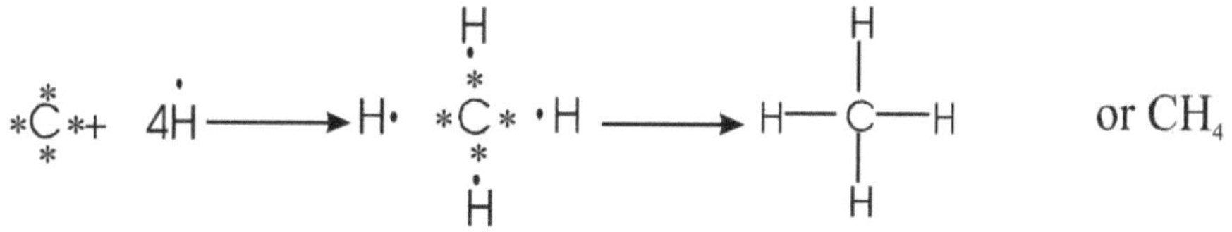

Note : Methane is the simplest hydrocarbon and is known as marsh gas.

Formation of Ethane (C_2H_6)

At.no. of C (Z) = 6, Electronic configuration of C = K (2) L (4)

At. no. of H(Z) = 1 Electronic configuration of H = K (1)

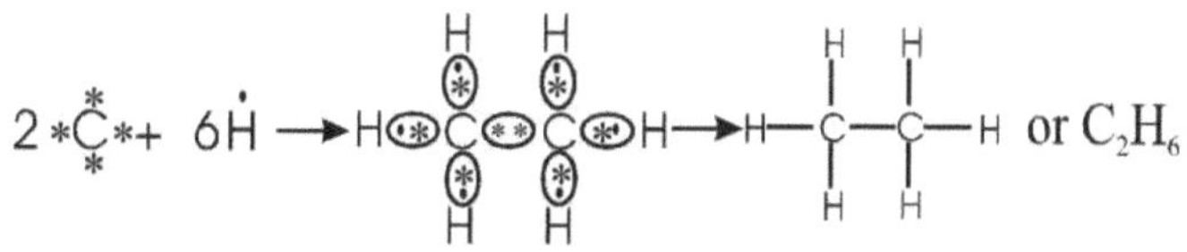

➤ **Double Covalent Bond:**

When two electrons from each atom are shared between two atoms a double covalent bond is formed. This bond is indicated by a double line (=) between two bonding atoms.

Formation of oxygen molecules :

At.no. of O (Z) = 8 Electronic configuration of O = K(2) L (6)

:Ö: + *Ö* ⟶ :Ö (:*) Ö* ⟶ :Ö=Ö* or O_2 (double bond is formed)

Shared electron pair

Formation of Acetylene (C_2H_4):

2 *C*+ 4H ⟶ H⊛C 8 C⊛H ⟶ H₂C=CH₂ (double bond) or C_2H_6

➤ **Triple Covalent Bond:**

When three electrons from each atom are shared between two atom a triple bond is formed. Some examples of triple covalent bond are C_2H_2 (acetylene), Hydrocyanic acid. **Formation of Nitrogen molecule:**

At. no. of N(Z)= 7 Electronic configuration of N = K(2) L(5)

N + :N: ⟶ N (*: *: *:) N ⟶ N≡N or (N_2 triple bond is formed)

Formation of Acetylene (C_2H_2):

2*C*+ 2H ⟶ H⊛C**C⊛H ⟶ H–C≡C–H or C_2H_2

(Triple bond)

Covalency : *Covalency of an element may be defined as :*

The number of electrons which an atom of the element shares with other atoms in the formation of covalent molecule.

For example :

- *In the molecules of H_2 and Cl_2, both the atoms have covalency of one.*
- *In the molecule of O_2, oxygen has covalency of two while in the molecules of N_2, nitrogen is trivalent.*
- *In the molecule of H_2O; oxygen has covalency of two while hydrogens is monovalent.*

Knowledge Enhancer

We have studied that the atoms take part in the formation of covalent bonds to acquire either two or eight electrons in the valence shell. However, there are many exceptions. In some cases, the central atom has less than eight electrons after sharing.

($BeCl_2$) (BF_3) ($AlCl_3$)

Similarly, in many other cases, the central atom acquires more than eight electrons after sharing.

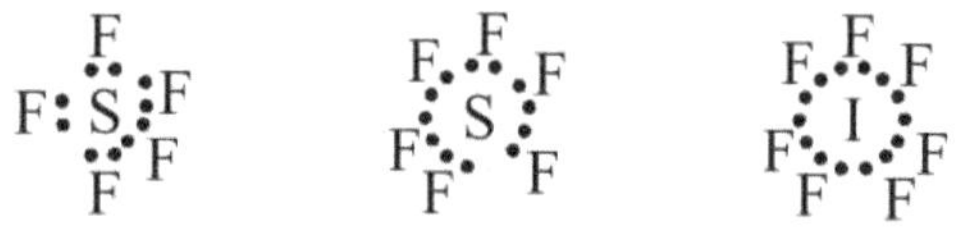

(PF_5) (SF_6) (IF_7)

4.3 ALLOTROPY

The property of an element as a result of which it exists in more than one form having different physical but same chemical properties is called **Allotropy**.

Carbon, Sulphur, phosphorus etc show allotropy.

Carbon exists in two different allotropic forms :

(i) Crystalline form. **Examples :** diamond, graphite and fullerene.

(ii) Non - crystalline or Amorphous form. **Examples :** coal, lampblack and charcoal.

Various allotropic forms of carbon are

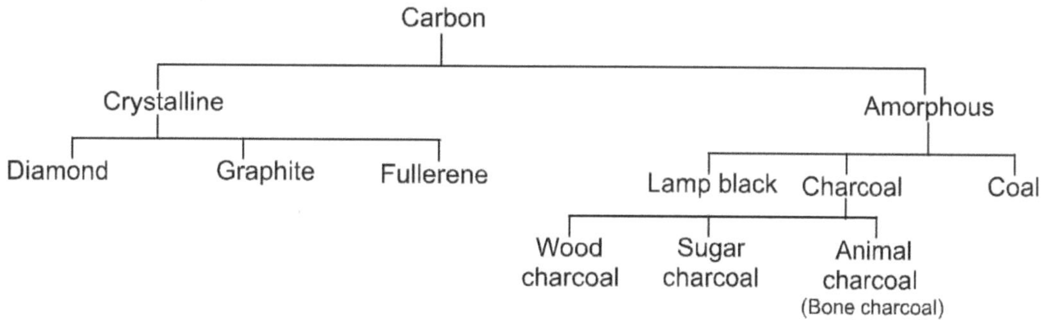

(1) Diamond :

Diamond is a beautiful crystalline allotrope of carbon. Its atomic symbol is C. The name 'diamond' has been taken from Greek words *diaphanes* (which means transparent) and *adamas* (which means indomitable or invincible) with reference to its extreme hardness.

(i) Structure of Diamond :

In a crystal of diamond, each carbon atom is bonded very strongly to four other carbon atoms in *tetrahedron* manner. The valency of each carbon atom is completely satisfied in diamond and there is no free electron. This arrangement of C-atoms makes diamond very hard, unreactive and bad conductor of electricity. The given figure depicts a portion of the diamond crystal. Smaller circles are representing C-atoms in tetrahedtral arrangement.

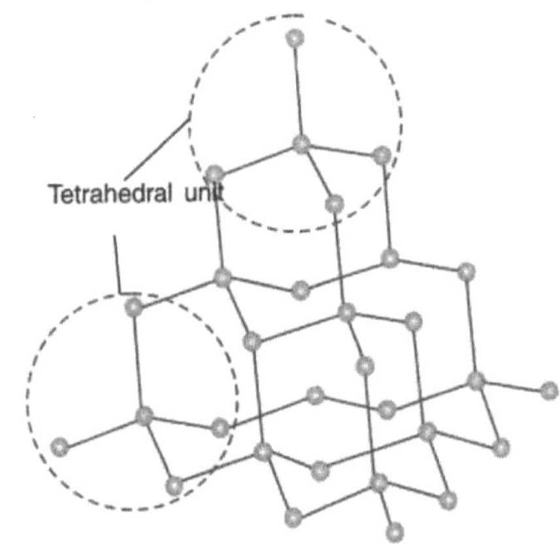

Figure : A portion of diamond structure

(ii) Properties of Diamond :

(A) Diamond is a transparent and colourless solid.

(B) Suitably cut and polished diamond sparkles brightly because it reflects most of the light (Refractive index of diamond is 2.45).

(C) The density of diamond is 3.51 g per cm^3 at 20°C.

(D) Diamond is the hardest natural substance known. Only a diamond can cut another diamond.

(E) It is a bad conductor of electricity.

(F) Melting point of dimond is 3550 ºC.

(G) Diamonds are not attacked by acids, alkalis and solvents like water, ether, benzene or carbon tetrachloride. But diamond is attacked by fluorine when heated to 750°C. The reaction results in the formation of carbon tetrafluoride.

$$\underset{\text{Carbon}}{C\,(\text{diamond})} + \underset{\text{Fluorine}}{2F_2} \xrightarrow{750\,°C} \underset{\text{Carbon tetrafluoride}}{CF_4}$$

(iii) Uses of Diamond :

(A) They are used in jewellery because of their ability to reflect and refract light.

(B) Diamonds are used in cutting glass and drilling rocks.

(C) Diamond has an extraordinary sensitivity to heat rays and due to this reason, it is used for making high precision thermometers.

(D) Diamond has the ability to cut out harmful radiations and due to this reason it is used for making protective windows for space probes.

(E) Diamond dies are used for drawing thin wires. Very thin tungsten wires of diameter less than one-sixth of the diameter of human hair have been drawn using diamond dies.

(F) Surgeons use diamond knives for performing delicate operations.

(2) GRAPHITE :

Graphite is the other crystalline allotropic form of carbon and occurs in free state in nature. It can also be prepared artificially by heating a mixture of sand and coke in electric furnance at about 3300 K.

- **Occurence of graphite:** Graphite occurs in free state in nature. It can be prepared artificially by heating a mixture of sand and coke in electric furnance at about 3300 K temperature.

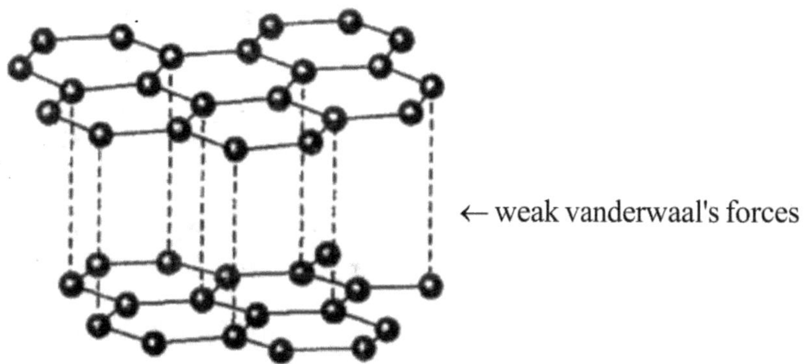

The Structure of Graphite

- **Structure:** In graphite each carbon atoms is linked to three other carbon atoms by single covalent bond resulting in hexagonal ring which are arranged in a layer. The C-C bond length is 1.42 Å. C-C bond angle is 120°. These layer are bonded together by weak Vander Waals force of attraction shown in figure by dotted lines. Distance between two layers is 3.35 Å.

- **Properties of Graphite :**
  - (i) Relatively soft and is greasy because of its hexagonal layer structure.
  - (ii) Has metallic lusture.
  - (iii) Colour varies from grey to black depends upon the origin.
  - (iv) Is opaque.
  - (v) Density varies from 2.0 to 2.25 gms/cm^3.
  - (vi) Melting point 3730ºC.

- **Uses of Graphite :**
  - (i) Graphite is used to make electrodes for electrolytic cells.
  - (ii) Being soft and greasy, it is used to lubricate the parts of machines.
  - (iii) Graphite crucibles can withstand very high temperature and can be used for melting substances with high melting points.
  - (iv) Graphite is also used to moderate the speed of the fast moving neutrons in nuclear reactors.
  - (v) Mixture with wax and clay, graphite is used for making cores of lead pencils as it can mark paper black. It is therefore, often called black lead or plumbago.

Differences between Diamond and Graphite

Property	Diamond	Graphite
1. Appearance	Transparent and colourless when pure	Dark grey and opaque
2. Crystal form	Tetrahedral giant structure	Hexagonal plates
3. Hardness	Hardest natural substance known	Soft and slippery
4. Impression	Does not mark paper	Leaves impression on paper
5. Conductivity (a) Electrical (b) Thermal	 Bad conductor Very high	 Good conductor Moderate
6. Density at 20 °C	3.51 g per cm^3	2.26 g per cm^3
7. Combustion	Burns in air above 900 °C and gives CO_2	Burns in air at about 700 °C and gives CO_2

(3) FULLERENE :

Fullerenes form another class of carbon allotropes. The first one to be identified was C-60 which has carbon atoms arranged in the shape of a football. Since this looked like the geodesic dome designed by the US architect Buckminster Fuller, the molecule was named fullerene.Buckminster fullerenes contain 60 carbon atoms arranged in round molecule resembling a soccer ball C_{60} molecule has marvelously symmetrical structure.

- It has spherical tomb like structure.
- The fullerene was named after the famous American architect Buckminster Fuller.
- In one molecule of fullerene there are 60, 70 or more carbon atoms present.
- C_{60} is the most stable fullerene which is also known as Buckminster fullerene.
- The structure of C_{60} has 32 faces in which 20 faces are hexagonal and 12 faces are pentagonal. Its structure is similar to football, therefore it is also known as bucky ball.
- C_{60} is a poor conductor of electricity. The C–C bond length is 1.40A.

- **Uses of Fullerene**
  - (i) Fullerenes in pure state act as insulators but can be converted to semi-conductors and super conductors under suitable conditions.
  - (ii) Bucky ball's ability of fullerenes to trap different atoms or molecules make them useful in the medical field. For example, radioactive C_{60} can be used in cancer as well as AIDS therapy.
  - (iii) Fullerenes help in improving antiwear and antifriction properties of lubricating oils.
  - (iv) Fullerenes in small amounts can catalyse the photochemical refining in industry.

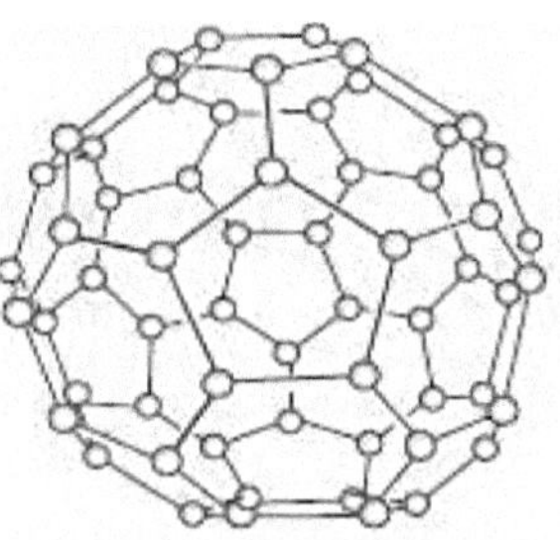

The structure of C-60

(i) ***There is another form of crystalline carbon knows as "white" carbon, but not much is known about it. Conditions such as temperature and pressure determine which allotrope of carbon occurs.***

(ii) ***Though non-metallic, graphite possesses a metallic luster. It is insoluble in ordinary solvent. Graphite is used in making electrodes in electric furnaces and electric ores. It is also used in lead pencils.***

(iii) ***Graphite is also used as an industrial lubricant because it possesses high melting point. Thus, no change is structure occurs even in if machineries are working at high temperatures and graphite there also serves as good lubricant.***

(iv) ***C60 molecule is a fused-ring of aromatic system containing 20 hexagons and 12 pentagons of C atoms. The five membered rings are connected to six membered rings while the six membered rings are fused to both five and six membered rings.***

Differences between graphite and Fullerene

Graphite	Fullerene
1. Graphite has extended crystal structure in which C-atoms are bonded in hexagonal layers. These layers are held by weak **Vander Waals forces**	1. Fullerene is a spherical molecule like a cage in which the C atoms are arranged in mixed hexagons and pentagons. In solid state these molecules are attached to each other by weak **Vander Waals forces**.
2. Graphite is insoluble in water, acids and any other solvent.	2. Fullerene is soluble in benzene and forms deep violet colour solution.
3. Graphite is a good conductor of electricity.	3.Crystalline fullerene has semi conducting properties.
4. The compounds of graphite with metals are called carbides. They are hard materials.	4. Compounds of fullerene with alkali metals are called fullerides and they are superconductors.

4.4 VERSATILE NATURE OF CARBON

The number of carbon compounds which are known today is approximately three million. This number exceeds the total number of compounds formed by all other elements. The five main reasons for this are as discussed below:

(i) **Catenation:** The property of self linking of carbon atoms through covalent bonds form long straight and branched chains and rings of different sizes is called **catenation**.

The property of catenation is probably due to :

(a) Small size

(b) Great strength of carbon-carbon bonds.

(ii) **Tetravalency of carbon :** Carbon belongs to group 14 of the periodic table. Since the atomic number of carbon is 6, the electronic configuration of carbon atom is 2,4. It has four electrons in the outermost shell. Therefore, its valency is four. Thus, carbon forms four covalent bonds in its compounds. A methane molecule (CH_4) is formed when four electrons of carbon are shared with four hydrogen atoms as shown below.

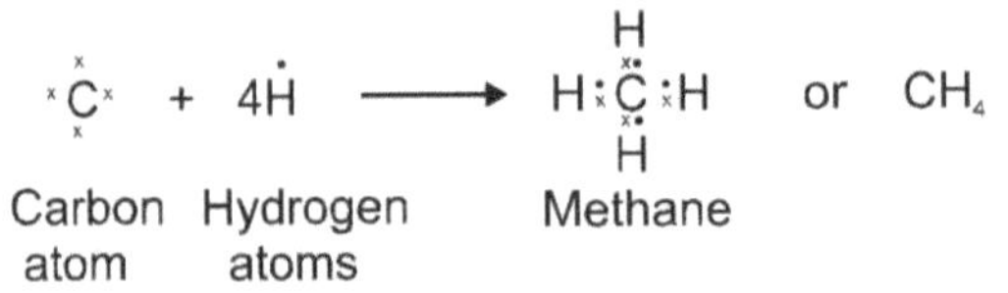

$$\dot{C} + 4\dot{H} \longrightarrow H:\overset{H}{\underset{H}{C}}:H \quad \text{or} \quad CH_4$$

Carbon atom, Hydrogen atoms, Methane

(iii) **Tendency to form multiple bonds :** Due to small size of carbon it has a strong tendency to form multiple bonds (double & triple bonds) by sharing more than one electron pair. As a result, it can form a variety of compounds. For example -

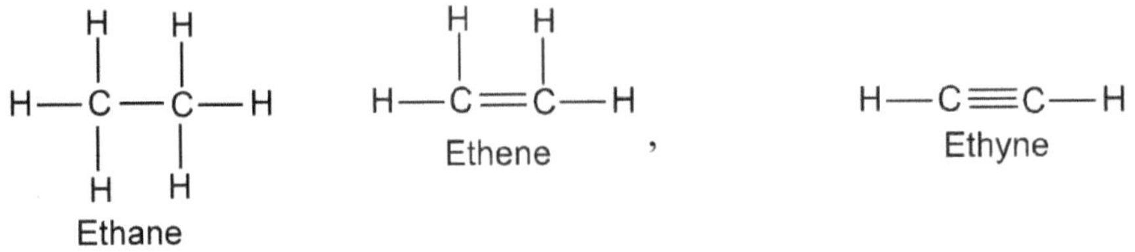

$$H-\underset{H}{\overset{H}{C}}-\underset{H}{\overset{H}{C}}-H \qquad H-\overset{H}{C}=\overset{H}{C}-H \qquad H-C\equiv C-H$$

Ethane, Ethene, Ethyne

(iv) **Isomerism:** Covalently bonded carbon compounds show isomerism. If a given molecular formula represents two or more structures having different properties is called **isomerism** and compounds are called **isomers**.

(v) **Tendency to Combine other hetero atom:** (like N, O, S, P, F, Cl, Br, I etc) :- Due to small size of carbon atom it can form very strong bonds with many elements such as O, N, S, F, Cl, Br, I, P etc.

Knowledge Enhancer

(i) A carbon atom attached to one other (or no other) carbon is called primary carbon (written as 1° carbon).

(ii) A carbon atom attached to two other carbon atoms is called secondary carbon (written as 2° carbon).

(iii) A carbon atom attached to three other carbon atoms is called tertiary carbon (written as 3° carbon).

(iv) A carbon atom attached to four other carbon atoms is called quarternary carbon (written as 4° carbon).

Hydrogen atoms attached to 1°, 2° and 3° carbon atoms are referred to as primary, secondary and tertiary H-atoms respectively. The following example clearly differentiates the various carbon atoms.

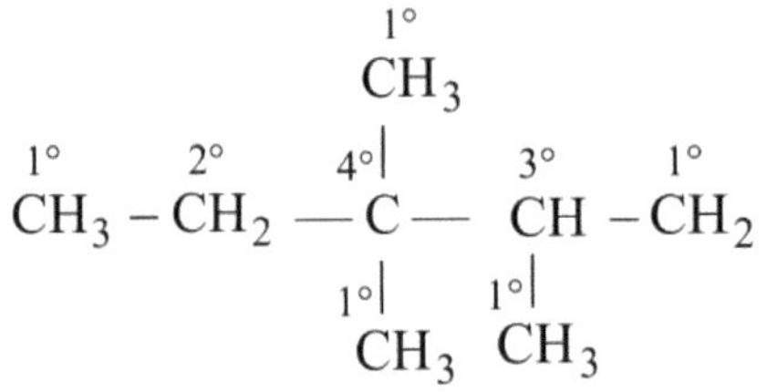

$$\overset{1^\circ}{CH_3}-\overset{2^\circ}{CH_2}-\underset{\underset{1^\circ}{CH_3}}{\overset{\overset{1^\circ}{CH_3}}{\overset{4^\circ}{C}}}-\underset{\underset{1^\circ}{CH_3}}{\overset{3^\circ}{CH}}-\overset{1^\circ}{CH_2}$$

Catenation is also present in silicon (Si) with atomic number (Z) equal to 14. Its valence shell electronic configuration (2, 8, 4) is similar to carbon. However, only seven to eight atoms of the element can be linked by covalent bonds. It is because of smaller bond dissociation energy of Si–Si bond (200 kJ mol^{-1}) as compared to that of C–C bond. Therefore, the bonds in the silicon atoms are not as strong as in carbon atoms.

4.5 ORGANIC COMPOUNDS

Compounds like urea, sugar, oils, fats, dyes, proteins, vitamin, hormones etc, which were isolated directly or indirectly from living organisms such as animals and plants are called **Organic compounds** and the branch of chemistry which deals with the study of these compounds called **Organic chemistry.**

Compounds like common salt (NaCl) blue vitriol $(CuSO_4 \cdot 5H_2O)$, green vitriol ($FeSO_4.7H_2O$) white vitriol ($ZnSO_4.7H_2O$), CaO, $Ca(OH)_2$ etc. which were isolated from non-living sources such as rocks and minerals are called **Inorganic compound** and the branch of chemistry which study about those compounds is called **Inorganic chemistry**.

- **Vital Force Theory :** According to this theory organic compounds are produced only under the influence of some mysterious force existing in the living organisms. This mysterious force was called the vital force. This theory was proposed by Berzelius in 1815.Since such vital force can not be created artificially, so organic compounds cannot be prepared artificialy in the laboratory.
- **Rejection of Vital force Theory :** In 1828 Wholer accidentlaly prepared urea by heating Potassium cyanate and Ammonium sulphate

$$\underset{\text{(Potassium Cyanate)}}{KCNO} + \underset{\text{(Ammonium sulphate)}}{(NH_4)_2SO_4} \longrightarrow \underset{\text{(Ammonium cyanate)}}{NH_4CNO} + \underset{\text{(Potassium sulphate)}}{K_2SO_4}$$

$$\underset{\text{(Potassium Cyanate)}}{KCNO} + \underset{\text{(Ammonium chloride)}}{NH_4Cl} \longrightarrow \underset{\text{(Ammonium cyanate)}}{NH_4CNO} + KCl$$

$$\underset{\text{(Ammonium cyanate)}}{NH_4CNO} \xrightarrow{\Delta} \underset{\text{(Urea)}}{H_2N-\overset{\overset{\displaystyle O}{\|}}{C}-NH_2}$$

(Inorganic Compound) (Organic Compound)

This synthesis discarded to vital force theory and clearly demonstrated that no mysterious force was required in the formation of organic compounds in the laboratory.

- **Modern definition of organic compound**: All covalent bonded carbon compounds (except oxides of carbon (CO, CO_2), carbonates, bicarbonates, (Metal Cyanides & carbides) are called **organic compound**.

CLASSIFICATION OF ORGANIC COMPOUNDS

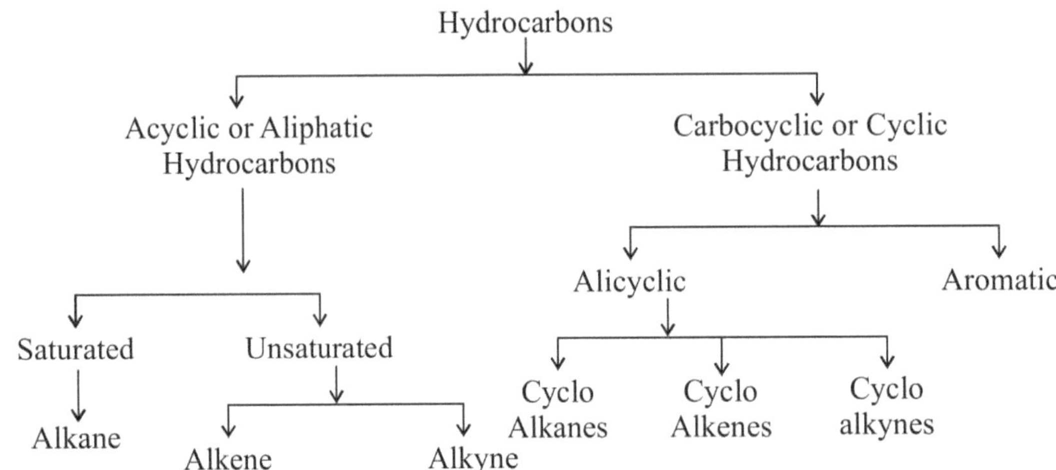

- **HYDROCARBONS**

Compounds made up of carbon and hydrogen are called hydrocarbons and all other compounds may be regarded to have been derived from them by replacement of one or more of their hydrogen atoms by other atom or group of atoms. These can be divide into two parts:

(a) ***Saturated Hydrocarbon :*** Compounds of carbon which have only single bonds between carbon atoms are called saturated compounds. These are also known as alkanes. Example- ethane, propane, methane etc. General formula for alkane is C_nH_{2n+2}.

(b) ***Unsaturated Hydrocarbon :*** Compounds of carbon which contain one or more double or triple bonds between C-C atoms are called unsaturated compounds. These compounds can be further divide into two parts:

(i) **Alkene:** If there is atleast one double bond between (C = C) such hydrocarbons are known as alkenes. Example of alkenes are Ethene (ethylene), Butene, Propene etc. General formula of alkene is C_nH_{2n}

(ii) **Alkyne:** If there is atleast one triple bond between (C ≡ C) such hydrocarbons are known as alkynes. Example of alkynes are Ethyne (acetylene), Butyne, Propyne etc. Alkynes are represented as C_nH_{2n-2}

Where n is the number of carbon atoms.

- **Open Chain Compound (Acyclic Compounds) and closed Chain (Cyclic Compounds) :**

  - **Open Chain Compounds:** The organic compounds in which the carbon atoms are linked to each other in such a manner that the molecules having an open chain structure are called **open chain** or **acyclic** or **aliphatic compound.** This may be of two types **straight chain** and **Branched chain** compound.

(i) Straight Chain :

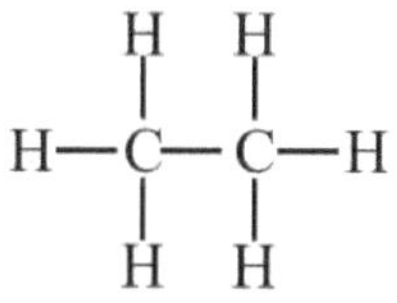

```
    H  H             H  H  H  H
    |  |             |  |  |  |
 H—C—C—H          H—C—C—C—C—H
    |  |             |  |  |  |
    H  H             H  H  H  H
```

Ethane (C_2H_6) 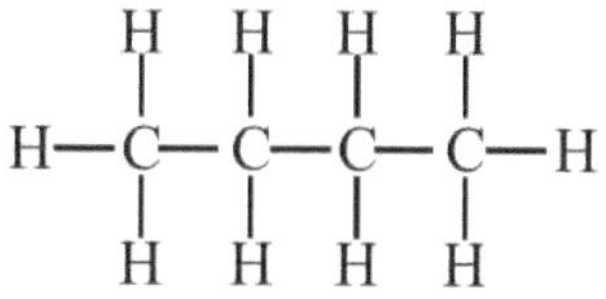 Propane (C_3H_8)

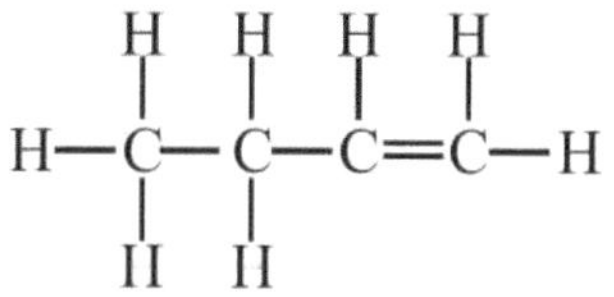

```
    H  H  H  H
    |  |  |  |
 H—C—C—C=C—H
    |  |
    H  H
```

Butene (C_4H_8)

(ii) Branched Chain :

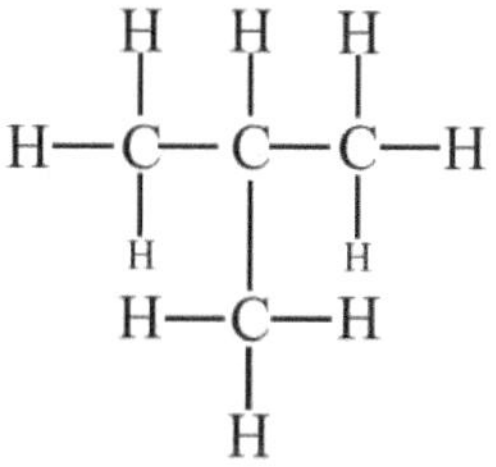

```
    H  H  H
    |  |  |
 H—C—C—C—H
    |  |  |
    H  |  H
    H—C—H
       |
       H
```

(2-methyl propane) or C_4H_{10} (Iso butane)

- **Closed Chain or Cyclic Compounds:** Compounds of carbon in, which carbon atoms are arranged in a ring are called **cylic compounds**.

  (a) Alicyclic Compounds : These compounds contain ring of three or more carbon atoms and resemble aliphatic compounds in characteristics. For example, cyclopropane (C_3H_6) can have the following ring structures which are all basically same but differ in presentation.

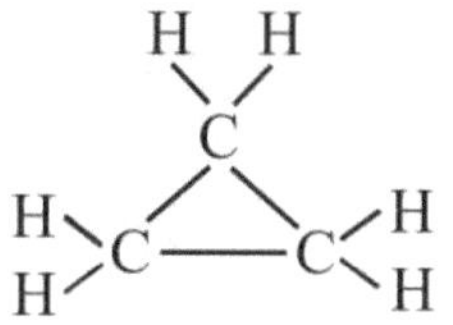

```
      H  H
       \/
       C                      CH2
  H   / \   H                 /  \
   >C————C<      or    H2C————CH2       or    △
  H          H
```

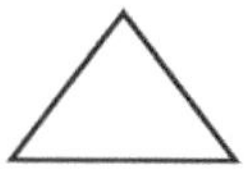

(Structural formula) (Condensed formula) (Bond line notation)

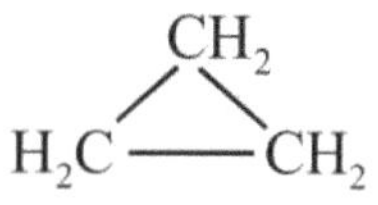

Cyclohexane (C_6H_{12}) another organic compound can be represented as follows :

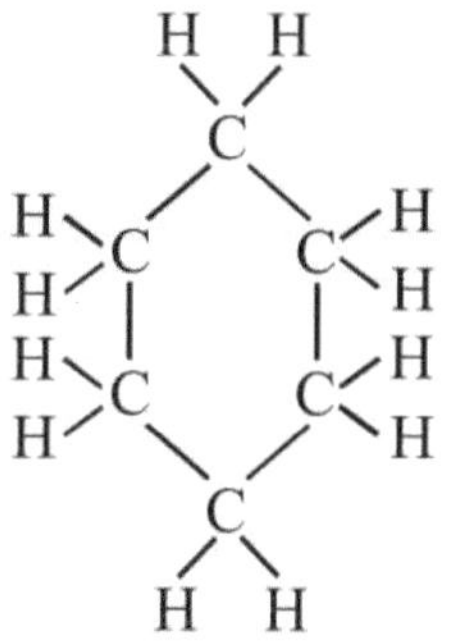

```
        H  H
         \/
         C                        CH2
   H   /   \   H               /     \
    >C       C<        or    H2C      CH2        or    ⬡
   H  |       |  H            |        |
   H  |       |  H           H2C      CH2
    >C       C<                \      /
   H   \   /   H                 CH2
         C
        /\
       H  H
```

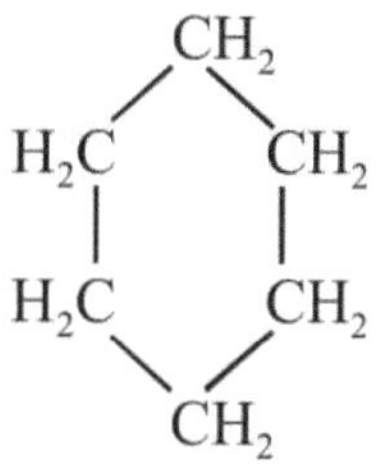

(Structural formula) (Condensed formula) (Bond line notation)

(b) Aromatic Compounds : Aromatic compounds are the cyclic compounds which contain in them one or more hexagonal rings of carbon atoms with three double bonds in the alternate positions. This is known as benzene ring.

(Structural formula) or (Condensed formula) or (Bond line notation)

These compounds are mostly represented by bond line notation. A few more example of the aromatic compounds are :

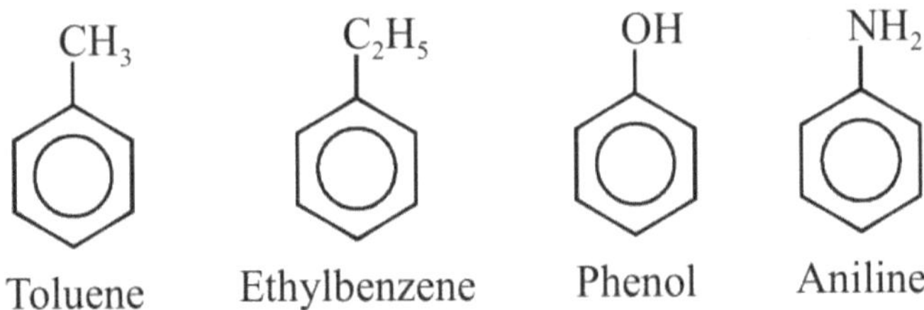

Toluene Ethylbenzene Phenol Aniline

(c) Heterocyclic compounds : Both alicyclic and aromatic compounds have rings of carbon atoms only. These are therefore, homocyclic in nature. In heterocyclic compounds, the ring may contain one or more atoms of either N, O or S etc. as its constituent. These are called heteroatoms. For example,

Pyrrole ; Furan ; Thiophene

➤ DERIVATIVES OF HYDROCARBON

If hydrogen of a hydrocarbon is displaced from other atoms or group of atoms such compounds are known as derivative of hydrocarbons. Examples are alcohol, ether, aldehyde etc. Such compounds can be divide into two parts:

(a) Hydrocarbon Group (Radical): When one hydrogen is removed from hydrocarbon rest species is known as hydrocarbon radical. It determines the physical properties of an organic compound. It is donated by **R**.

On the basis of parent hydrocarbon it can be named as below:

Hydrocarbon	Formula	Name of radical	Formula
Alkane	C_nH_{2n+2}	Alkyl group	C_nH_{2n+1}
Alkene	C_nH_{2n}	Alkenyl group	C_nH_{2n-1}
Alkyne	C_nH_{2n-2}	Alkynyl group	C_nH_{2n-3}

(b) **Functional Groups**: An atom or a group of atoms which displaces the hydrogen atom from hydrocarbon molecule is called **Functional Group.** It determines the characteristic chemical properties of an organic compound. It is denoted by **G**. Some examples of function group are given below. All compounds with same functional group belong the same family. **Example:-** Alcohol family contains -OH group.

Formula of unction group	Name of Functional group	Types of organic compound	Family
— Cl	Chloro	R-Cl	Halogen
— Br	Bromo	R-Br	Halogen
— I	Iodo	R-I	Halogen
— F	Floro	R-F	Halogen
— OH	Hydroxyl	R-OH	Alcohol
H—C(=O)—	Aldehyde	R-CHO	Aldehyde
>C=O	Ketone	$R_2C=O$	Ketone
—C(=O)—OH	Carboxyl	R-COOH	Carboxylic acid
— NH_2	Amino	RNH_2	Amine
—OR	Alkoxy	R-O-R	ether
—C(=O)—OR	Ester	R-COOR	Ester

4.6 HOMOLOGOUS SERIES

A homologous series may, thus, be defined as a group of structurally similar compounds each member of which differs from the proceeding or succeeding, member by CH_2. The members of a series are called **homologous**.

➤ **Characteristics of Homologous Series**

(i) All members of a particular homologous series can be represented by the general formula. For example, alkane (C_nH_{2n+2}), alkenes (C_nH_{2n}) and alkynes (C_nH_{2n-2}).

(ii) Each member of the homologous series differs from the members above or below the series only by one CH_2 group.

(iii) The molecular weight of two adjacent members of a homologous series differs by 14 (i.e., $CH_2 = (12 \times 1) + (1 \times 2) = 14$).

(iv) All members of a homologous series can be prepared by the same general methods.

(v) All members of a homologous series have same chemical properties due to same functional group.

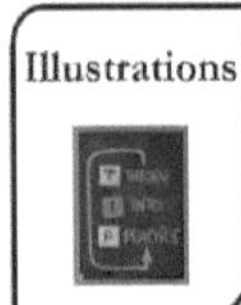

Illustration 1

Name some organic compounds with oxygen containing functional groups that have been derived from methane.

Solution

Methane (CH_4) is the simplest saturated hydrocarbon. When one hydrogen atom of methane is replaced by a functional group, a compound belonging to the characteristic family of the functional group is obtained. Various compounds containing different functional groups obtained from methane are given below

$H-C(H)(H)-H$ —H-replaced by –OH→ $H-C(H)(H)-OH$ or CH_3OH **(Methanol)**

$H-C(H)(H)-H$ —H-replaced by –COOH→ $H-C(H)(H)-COOH$ or CH_3COOH **(Ethanoic Acid)**

$H-C(H)(H)-H$ —H-replaced by $-\overset{O}{\overset{\|}{C}}-OCH_3$→ $H-C(H)(H)-\overset{O}{\overset{\|}{C}}-OCH_3$ or CH_3COOCH_3 **(Methyl ethanoate)**

4.7 NOMENCLATURE OF ORGANIC COMPOUND

Naming of organic compound is called nomenclature. There are two main systems of Nomenclature.

(1) TRIVIAL SYSTEM OR COMMON NAMES

These name were given after the source from which the organic compounds were first isolated.

- Acetic acid (CH_3COOH) got its name from acetum (means vinegar) because it is present in vinegar.
- Formic acid (HCOOH) got its name from formica (means red ant) because it is present in Red ant.
- Marsh gas (CH_4) got its name because it is obtained from marshy land.

S.N.	Organic Compound	Trivial Name	Source
1.	CH_3OH	Wood spirit or Methyl spirit	Obtained by destructive distillation of wood.
2.	NH_2CONH_2	Urea	Obtained from urine.
3.	CH_4	Marsh gas (Fire damp)	It was produced in marsh places.
4.	CH_3COOH	Vinegar	Obtained from Acetum - i.e. Vinegar.
5.	$COOH - COOH$ (COOH above, COOH below, joined by a bond)	Oxalic acid	Obtained from oxalis plant.
6.	HCOOH	Formic acid	Obtained from formicus (Red ant)
7.	$CH_3 - CH(OH) - COOH$	Lactic acid	Obtained from sour milk.
8.	$CH_2COOH - CH(OH)COOH$ (CH_2COOH above, $CH(OH)COOH$ below, joined by a bond)	Malic acid	Obtained from apples.
9.	$CH_3CH_2CH_2COOH$	Butyric acid	Obtained from butter.
10.	$CH_3(CH_2)_4COOH$	Caproic acid	Obtained from goats

(2) IUPAC NAME:

In order to solve the problem of naming of organic compounds, organisation called international chemical congress for the first time met at Geneva in 1892. They developed a certain system called Geneva system. Since then the system of naming has been improved from time to time by the International union of pure and Applied chemistry and the new system is called IUPAC system of naming. This system of nomenclature was introduced in 1947. This latest IUPAC system is based on the recommendation made in 1993.

The IUPAC name of any organic compound can be derived by using the following rules. It mainly consist of three parts :

(i) Word Root (ii) Suffix (iii) Prefix

(i) Word Root: The number of carbon atoms present in the linear continuous chain (main chain or present chain) of the molecule is denoted by word Root.

It is generally indicated as 'alk'

Chain length	Word Root (Alk)
One carbon (C_1)	Meth
Two Carbon (C_2)	Eth
Three Carbon (C_3)	Prop
Four Carbon (C_4)	But
Five Carbon (C_5)	Pent
Six Carbon (C_6)	Hex
Seven Carbon (C_7)	Hept
Eight Carbon (C_8)	Oct
Nine Carbon (C_9)	Non
Ten Carbon (C_{10})	Dec
Eleven carbon (C_{11})	Undec
Twelve carbon (C_{12})	Dodec

(ii) **Suffix :**Suffixes are of two types : primary and secondary suffixes.

(a) ***Primary Suffix:*** Primary suffix is always added after the word root to indicate whether carbon chain is saturated or unsaturated.

	Nature of Carbon Chain	Primary suffix	Name
(i)	Saturated i.e. Contain C – C single covalent bond only	ane	Alkane
(ii)	Unsaturated i.e. Contains at least one C = C double covalent bond	ene	Alkene
(iii)	Unsaturated i.e. Contain at least one C ≡ C triple covalent bond	yne	Alkyne

(b) ***Secondary Suffix*:** Secondary suffix is added after primary suffix to indicate the presence of particular functional group in the carbon chain.

While adding secondary suffix to the primary suffix, the terminal 'e' of the primary suffix (i.e. ane, ene, yne) is dropped if secondary suffix begins with vowels **(a, e, i, o, u)** but it is retained if the secondary suffix begins with consonant.

Family	Functional Group	Secondary suffix	IUPAC Name
Alcohol	—O—H	—ol	Alkane-ol=Alkanol
Aldehyde	$-\underset{\underset{O}{\parallel}}{C}-H$	—al	Alkane-al = Alkanal
Ketone	$R-\underset{\underset{O}{\parallel}}{C}-R'$	—one	Alkane-one = Alkanone
Carboxylic acid	$-\underset{\underset{O}{\parallel}}{C}-OH$	—oic acid	Alkane-oic acid = Alkanoic acid
Amine	$-NH_2$	—amine	Alkane-amine = Alkanamine
Amide	$-\overset{\overset{O}{\parallel}}{C}-NH_2$	–amide	Alkane-amide = Alkanamide
Cyanides	$-C\equiv N$	—nitrile	Alkane + nitrile = Alkane nitrile
Ester	$-\overset{\overset{O}{\parallel}}{C}-O-R$	Alkyl-oate	Alkyl/ Alkane-oate = Alkyl alkanoate

Ex. 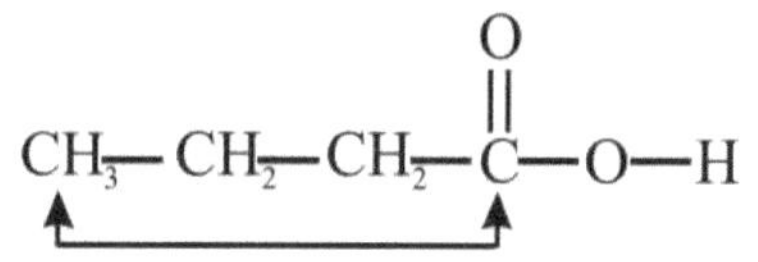 $CH_3-CH_2-CH_2-\overset{\overset{O}{\parallel}}{C}-O-H$

Linear Continuous Chain :

Family - Carboxylic acid; Word Root = 4, Carbon atom i.e. '**But**' primary Suffix - '**ane**'.

Functional group i.e. secondary suffix = oic acid

Hence name is, But + ane + oic acid = Butanoic acid

Groups given below does not have any Suffix :

Ether	– OR	alkoxy
Epoxide	– O –	epoxy
Azo	– N = N –	azo
Nitroso	– NO	nitroso
Halogen	– X (F, Cl, Br, I)	halo

S.N.	Functional group	Prefix / Suffix	Example
1.	Alkyl group (as a side chain)	Prefix-Alkyl	$H_3C-CH(CH_3)-CH_3$ (Methylpropane)
2.	Halogen	Prefix – chloro, bromo etc.	$H_3C-CH_2-CH_2-Cl$ (1-Chloropropane)
			$H_3C-CHBr-CH_3$ (2-Bromopropane)
3.	Alcohol	Suffix - ol	$H_3C-CH_2-CH_2-OH$ (Propan-1-ol)
4.	Aldehyde	Suffix - al	$H_3C-CH_2-CH=O$ (Propanal)
5.	Ketone	Suffix - one	$H_3C-C(=O)-CH_3$ (Propanone)
6.	Carboxylic acid	Suffix - oic acid	$H_3C-CH_2-C(=O)-OH$ (Propanoic acid)
7.	Double bond (alkenes)	Suffix - ene	$H_3C-CH=CH_2$ (Prop-1-ene)
8.	Triple bond (alkynes)	Suffix - yne	$H_3C-C\equiv C-H$ (Prop-1-yne)

If both double and triple bonds are present, the double bond is always, given preference over the triple bond.
For example,

$$\overset{5}{\underset{1}{HC}} \equiv \overset{4}{\underset{2}{C}} - \overset{3}{\underset{3}{CH_2}} - \overset{2}{\underset{4}{CH}} = \overset{1}{\underset{5}{CH_2}}$$

1 ← Correct numbering (top row: 5 4 3 2 1)
5 ← Incorrect numbering (bottom row: 1 2 3 4 5)

Priority order :

Functional group > $>C=C<$ > $>-C\equiv C-$ > $>$Substituent

Note: $-\overset{O}{\overset{\|}{C}}-OH$, $-\overset{O}{\overset{\|}{C}}-H$, $-\overset{O}{\overset{\|}{C}}-NH_2$, $-\overset{O}{\overset{\|}{C}}-O-R$, $-C\equiv N$

Functional group containing carbon always get number one during carbon chain numbering, hence their location is not require to write in the IUPAC name.

(iii) ***Prefix:*** Prefix is added before word root to indicate side chains or substituents group present in the linear carbon chain of the molecule.

(a) **Primary Prefix:** A primary prefix "cyclo" is used in order to differentiate a cyclic compound from an acyclic compound.
For example,

$CH_3-CH_2-CH_3$
Propane

H_2C—CH_2 (ring with CH_2)
Cyclopropane

$CH_3-CH_2-CH_2-CH_3$
Butane

H_2C—CH_2 / H_2C—CH_2 (ring)
Cyclobutane

(b) **Secondary Prefix:** In the IUPAC system of nomenclature, certain characteristic groups are not considered as or secondary suffixes. These are regarded as substituents and are denoted by secondary prefixes. The secondary prefixes of a few substituents are given.

Group	Secondary Prefix
—F	Fluoro
— Cl	Chloro
—Br	Bromo
—I	Iodo
$—NO_2$	Nitro
—O—R [R(CH_3,C_2H_5 etc.)]	Alkoxy (methoxy (O-CH_3) Ethoxy (O-C_2H_5)
R — (CH_3, —C_2H_5)	Alkyl [methyl (CH_3), Ethyl (C_2H_5)]
—NO	Nitroso
—C_6H_5	Phenyl

➢ **Rules for IUPAC nomenclature of organic compounds**

There are certain (following) rule for naming a complex organic molecule according to IUPAC system. These rules are illustrated below.

1. **Longest Chain Rule :** The first step for naming an organic compound is to select the longest continuous chain of carbon atoms which may or may not be horizontal (straight). This is called the parent chain or main chain, and other carbon chains attached to it are known as side chains. On the basis of the number of carbon atoms present in the parent chain, the parent hydrocarbon is determined. For example, if the parent chain contains six carbon atoms, the compound is considered to be a derivative of hexane.

   Example : The structure I has the longest chain of six carbon atoms present in a straight line; therefore it is said to be a derivative of hexane. On the other hand, in structure II the straight chain has only four or three carbon atoms while the longest possible chain may have as many as six carbon atoms (zig-zig chain).

```
            C
            |
C – C – C – C – C – C
```

I
(Longest chain, straight)

```
C – C – C – C
        |
        C – C – C
```

II
(Longest chain, zig-zig)

Therefore, both the structures are the derivatives of hexane.

In case a molecule contains two equally long carbon chains, the one carrying larger number of side chains is selected. For example, structure A and B have carbon chains of equal lengths (C_7), but the one carrying three substituents is selected.

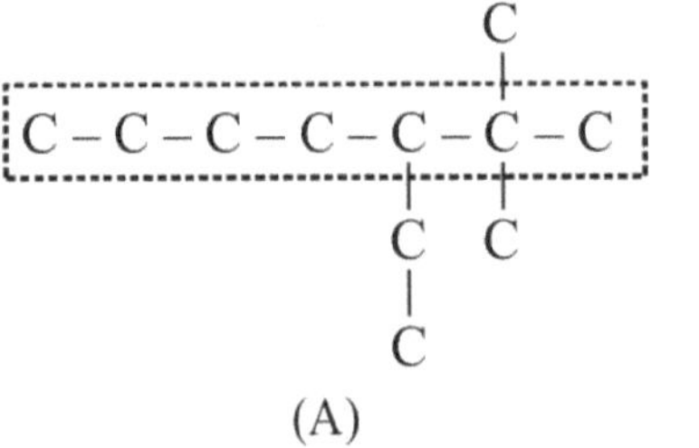

(A)
Straight parent chain of C_7
with three side chains (correct)

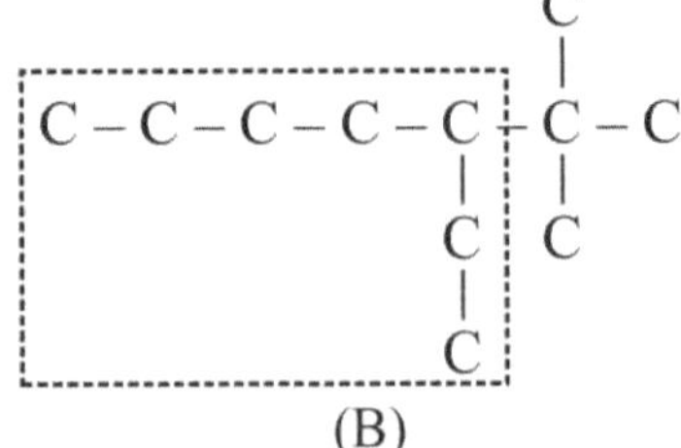

(B)
Zig-zig parent chain of C_7
with only one side chains (incorrect)

2. **Lowest number of lowest sum rule :** The carbon atom of longest carbon chain is numbered as 1, 2, 3, 4, ... etc. starting from the end that gives the lowest possible number to the substituent. For example, in structures A and B numbering may be done in two ways;

```
      X                          X
      |                          |
C–C–C–C–C–C                C–C–C–C–C–C
1 2 3 4 5 6                6 5 4 3 2 1
```

Substituent at C_3(A) (Correct)   Substituent at C_4(B) (Incorrect)

In one case (A), the substituent is assigned position 3 while in other case (B), it is assigned position 4. Hence the former, being smaller, is correct. The number that locates the position of a substituent is known as locant. Thus the locant for X in the above correct structure is 3.

In case, the parent chain has two or more substituents, numbering must be done in such a way that the sum of the locants on the parent chain is the lowest possible. Thus in following structures A and B numbering may be done in two ways: in one (A), the sum of locants is 9 while in other (B), it is 12, hence the former is correct while the later is wrong.

```
    C C C                      C C C
    | | |                      | | |
C–C–C–C–C–C                C–C–C–C–C–C
1 2 3 4 5 6                6 5 4 3 2 1
```

Sum of locants: $2 + 3 + 4 = 9$ (A) (Correct)   Sum of locants: $3 + 4 + 5 = 12$ (B) (Incorrect)

3. **Name of the complex alkane :** The name of the substituent is prefixed to the name of the parent hydrocarbon and its position on the main chain is indicated by writing the locant before the prefix. A hypen (–) is inserted between the locant and the substituent name. The final name is always written as one word. Thus the following compound is written as 2-methylpentane.

```
         CH3
         |
CH3 – CH – CH2 – CH2 – CH3
 1     2     3     4     5
```

2–Methylpentane

4. **Alphabetical order of sides chains :** In case two or more alkyl groups (side-chains) are attached to the parent chain, these are prefixed in alphabetic order, e.g.

```
CH3 – CH3 – CH – CH2 – CH3
       |     |
      CH3   C2H5
```

3–Ethyl–2methylpentane and not as
2–Methyl-3-ethylpentane

5. **If a substituent is present two or more times :** This is indicated by the prefix di-,tri-, tetra-, etc. added to the substituent. The different locants of the substituents are separated by commas. For example,

$$\begin{array}{ccccccccc} & & CH_3 & & CH_3 & & & & \\ 1 & & 2| & & 3| & & 4 & & 5 \\ CH_3 & - & CH & - & CH & - & CH_2 & - & CH_3 \end{array}$$

2,3–Dimethylpentane

$$\begin{array}{ccccccccccc} & & & & CH_3 & & & & & & \\ 6 & & 5 & & 4| & & 3 & & 2 & & 1 \\ CH_3 & - & CH_2 & - & CH_3 & - & CH_2 & - & C & - & CH_3 \\ & & & & | & & & & | & & \\ & & & & C_2H_5 & & & & CH_3 & & \end{array}$$

4–Ethyl–2,4–Dimethylhexane

6. **Naming the complex substituent :** In case the substituent on the parent chain is complex (i.e. it has itself branched chain) then it is named as a substituted alkyl group and its carbon chain is numbered from the carbon atom attached to the main chain. The name of this complex substituent is written in bracket to avoid confusion with the numbers of the main chain. e.g.,

$$\begin{array}{ccccccccccccccccc} & & & & & & & & {}^{3'}CH_3 & & & & & & & & \\ & & & & & & & & | & & & & & & & & \\ & & & & & & & & {}^{2'}CH-CH_3 & & & & & & & & \\ & & & & & & & & | & & & & & & & & \\ & & & & & & & & {}^{1'}CH-CH_3 & & & & & & & & \\ 1 & & 2 & & 3 & & 4 & & 5| & & 6 & & 7 & & 8 & & 9 \\ CH_3 & - & CH_2 & - & CH_2 & - & CH_2 & - & CH_2 & - & CH_2 & - & CH_2 & - & CH_2 & - & CH_3 \end{array}$$

5–(1',2'–dimethylpropyl)–nonane

Knowledge Enhancer

When two or more substituents are present, the carbon atoms of parent chain are numbered in such a way that the set of locants is the lowest. This is called lowest set of locants rule.

In accordance with the above rules, the carbon atoms of the alkanes given below should be numbered as shown in structures A and not as in structures B.

$$\begin{array}{ccccccccc} & & \overset{2}{C}H_2\overset{1}{C}H_3 & & & & & & \\ & & |3 & & 4 & & & & \\ CH_3 & - & CH & - & CH & - & CH_2 & - & CH_3 \\ & & & & 5| & & & & \\ & & & & \overset{5}{C}H_2\overset{6}{C}H_2\overset{7}{C}H_3 & & & & \end{array}$$

A(Correct)
Sum of the locants =3 + 4 = 7
Set of locants = 3, 4

$$\begin{array}{ccccccccc} & & \overset{6}{C}H_2\overset{7}{C}H_3 & & & & & & \\ & & |5 & & 4 & & & & \\ CH_3 & - & CH & - & CH & - & CH_2 & - & CH_3 \\ & & & & 3| & & & & \\ & & & & CH_2\overset{2}{C}H_2\overset{1}{C}H_3 & & & & \end{array}$$

B(Correct)
Sum of the locants =4 + 5 = 9
Set of locants = 4, 5

Thus, according to the lowest sum rule, the numbering of the carbon chain should be done from right to left but according to the lowest set of locants rule, the numbering should be done from left to right. To overcome such an ambiguity, the IUPAC nomenclature recommends that the lowest set of locants rule should be preferred over the lowest sum rule.

Illustration 2

Give IUPAC name of the following compounds

W.R. = Word root, P.S. = Primary suffix, S.S. = Secondary suffix

1. $H_3C-CH_2-CH_2-OH$

   Word root - Prop; Primary suffix - ane

   Functional group (Secondary suffix) = l-position of OH group in carbon chain

   Hence IUPAC Name is, **1- Prop + ane - e + ol = 1-propanol**

2. $CH_3-CH_2-CH=CH_2$

   Word Root - but Primary Suffix = ene Position - 1

   Name: **1-Butene**

3. $\underset{3}{CH_3}-\underset{2}{CH_2}-\underset{1}{\overset{\overset{O}{||}}{C}}-OH$

   W.R. - Prop, P.S. = ane Secondary Suffix = Oic acid Position - 1

   Name: **Propanoic Acid**

4. $\underset{4}{CH_3}-\underset{3}{CH_2}-\underset{2}{\overset{\overset{O}{||}}{C}}-\underset{1}{CH_3}$

   W.R. = But. P.S. = ane S.S. = one Position-2

   Name: **2-Butanone**

5. $\underset{4}{CH_3}-\underset{3}{CH_2}-\underset{2}{CH_2}-\underset{1}{\overset{\overset{O}{||}}{C}}-H$

   W.R. = But., P.S. = ane, S.S. = al Position-1

   Name : **Butanal**

6. $\underset{4}{CH_3}-\underset{3}{CH_2}-\underset{2}{\overset{\overset{Cl}{|}}{CH}}-\underset{1}{CH_3}$ **2- Chlorobutane**

7. $\underset{4}{CH_3}-\underset{3}{C}\equiv\underset{2}{C}-\underset{1}{CH_3}$ **2 - Butyne**

8. 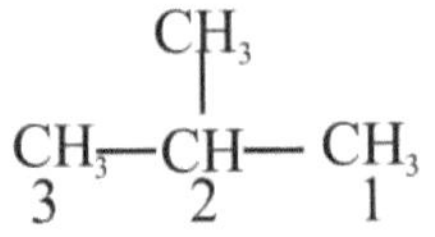 $\underset{3}{CH_3}-\underset{2}{\overset{\overset{CH_3}{|}}{CH}}-\underset{1}{CH_3}$ **2- Methyl propane or Methyl propane**

9. 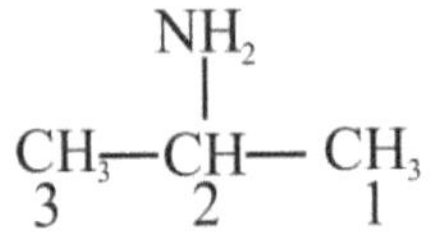 $\underset{3}{CH_3}-\underset{2}{\overset{\overset{NH_2}{|}}{CH}}-\underset{1}{CH_3}$ **2- Propanamine**

10. 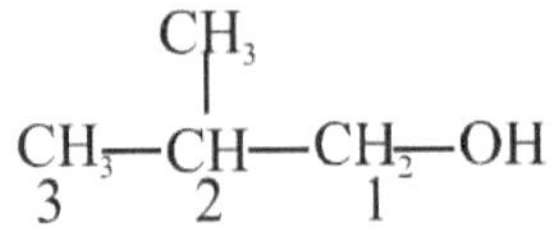 $\underset{3}{CH_3}-\underset{2}{\overset{\overset{CH_3}{|}}{CH}}-\underset{1}{CH_2}-OH$ **2-Methyl-1-propanol**

11. 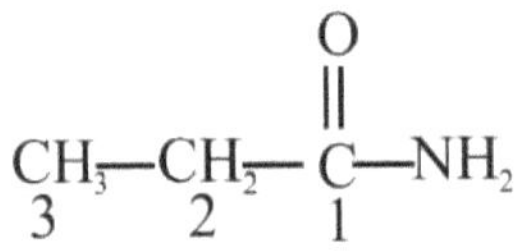 $\underset{3}{CH_3}-\underset{2}{CH_2}-\underset{1}{\overset{\overset{O}{||}}{C}}-NH_2$ **Propanamide**

12. 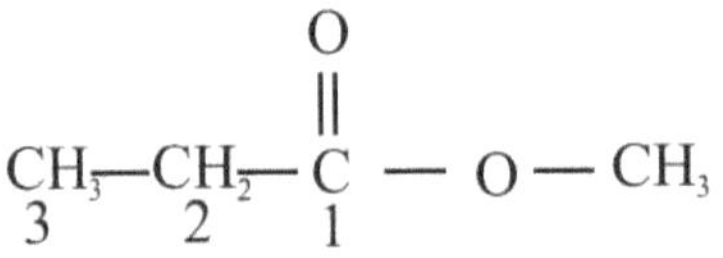 $\underset{3}{CH_3}-\underset{2}{CH_2}-\underset{1}{\overset{\overset{O}{||}}{C}}-O-CH_3$ **Methyl propanoate**

Illustration 3

Write IUPAC names of following compound:

1. 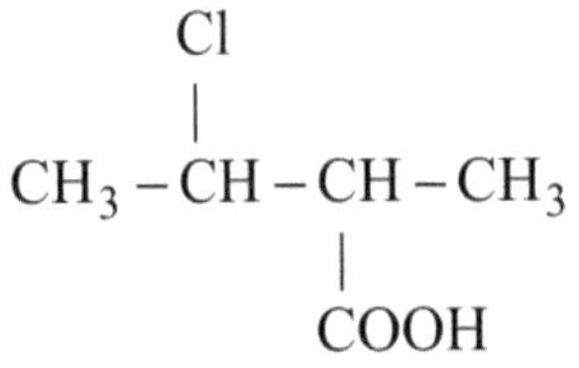 $CH_3-\overset{\overset{Cl}{|}}{CH}-\underset{\underset{COOH}{|}}{CH}-CH_3$

2. 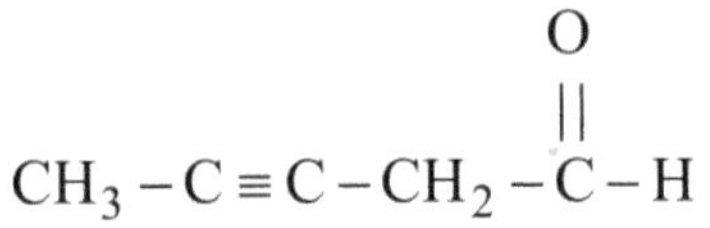 $CH_3-C\equiv C-CH_2-\overset{\overset{O}{||}}{C}-H$

3. $CH_3-\underset{\underset{OH}{|}}{\overset{\overset{CH_3}{|}}{C}}-\overset{\overset{O}{||}}{C}-CH_3$

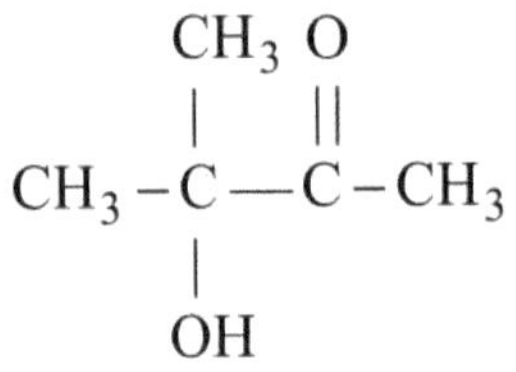

4. 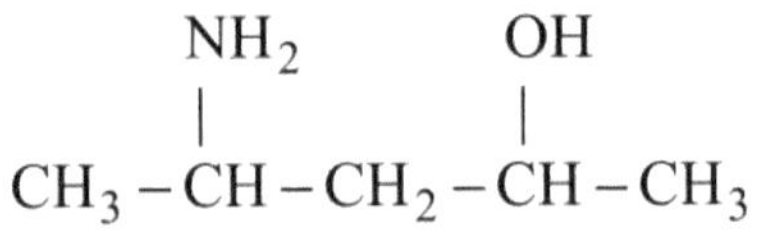 $CH_3-\overset{\overset{NH_2}{|}}{CH}-CH_2-\overset{\overset{OH}{|}}{CH}-CH_3$

5. 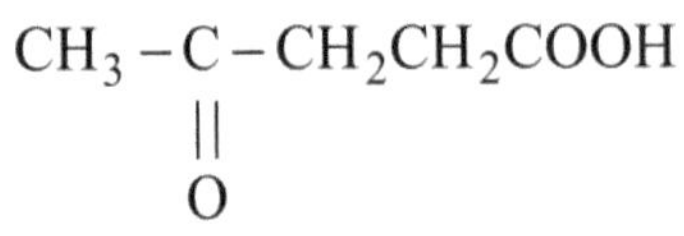 $CH_3-\underset{\underset{O}{||}}{C}-CH_2CH_2COOH$

Solution

1. 3-chloro-2-methylbutan-1-oic acid
2. Pent-3-yn-1-al
3. 3-Hydroxy-3-methylbutan-2-one
4. 4-Aminopentane-2-ol
5. 4-Oxopentanoic acid

4.8 ISOMERISM

Definition: Compounds having same molecular formula show different physical and chemical properties are called isomers and the phenomenon is called isomerism.

The difference in properties of isomers is due to the difference in the relative arrangements of various atoms present in their molecules. Organic compound show following types of structural isomersim on the basis of their difference in structural arrangement of atoms.

➢ **Type of Isomerism**

The following figure shows the pictorial representation of different types of isomerism

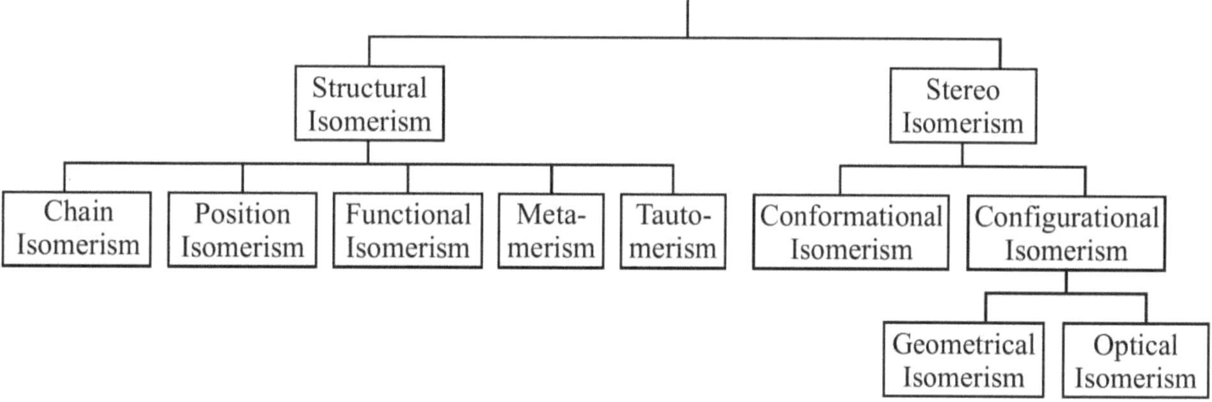

Structural Isomerism In this type of isomerism the isomers have different molecular structure due to the different arrangement of atoms in their molecules.

➤ **Chain isomerism :** Organic compounds having same molecular formula but difference in the nature of length carbon chain are called **chain isomers**.

For example, Let us consider the molecular formula of an alkane C_4H_{10}.

$CH_3-CH_2-CH_2-CH_3$
Butane
(Here linear chain contains 4 carbon atom)

$CH_3-CH(CH_3)-CH_3$
(2-Methylpropane)
(Here the linear chain contains 3 carbon atom)

➤ **Position isomerism :** Compounds having same molecular formula but differ in the position of functional group, double bond or triple bond in the carbon chain are called **position isomers**. This type of isomerism is shown by Alkene, Alkyne, Alcohol, Amine, Haloalkane etc.

Ex.1 Let us consider the molecular formula of an alcohol $(C_nH_{2n+2}O)$ C_3H_8O

$CH_3-CH_2-CH_2-OH$
(1-Propanol)

$\underset{3}{CH_3}-\underset{2}{CH(OH)}-\underset{1}{CH_3}$
(2-Propanol)

The difference only in the position of —OH group in the linear Carbon chain.

Ex.2 Let us consider the molecular formula of alkene C_4H_8 (C_nH_{2n})

$H_2C = CH—CH_2—CH_3$ (1 - Butene) $CH_3—CH = CH—CH_3$ (2- Butene)

They are differ in the position of double bond in the linear carbon chain.

(i) Chain isomerism is observed when the number of carbon atoms is four or more than four in an organic compounds. Chain isomers differ in the nature of carbon chain, i.e. in the length of the carbon chain.

(ii) The isomers showing chain isomerism belong to the some homologous series, i.e. functional group, class of the compound (cyclic or open) remains unchanged.

(iii) Aldehydes, carboxylic acids (and their derivatives) and cyanides do not exhibit positional isomerism.

(iv) Chain and positional isomerism cannot be possible together between two isomerism compounds. If two compounds are chain isomers then these two will not be positional isomers.

➤ **Functional isomerism :** Compounds having same molecular formula but differ in nature of functional group are called functional isomers.

Ex.1 Alcohol and ether have same molecular formula ($C_nH_{2n+2}O$) but have different functional group hence show functional isomerism. C_2H_6O

$CH_3—CH_2—OH$ (Ethanol) $CH_3—O—CH_3$ (Methoxy methane)

Ex.2 Aldehyde and Ketone having same molecular formula ($C_nH_{2n}O$) C_3H_6O

$CH_3—CH_2—C(=O)—H$ (Propanal) $CH_3—C(=O)—CH_3$ (Propanone)

Illustration 4

Which type of isomerism following pair of compound represents?

$CH_3-C(=O)-OH$ (Acetic acid) and 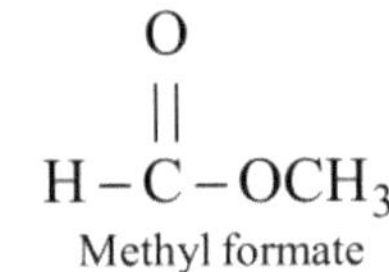

$H-C(=O)-OCH_3$ (Methyl formate)

Solution

Above pair of compounds represents functional isomerism.

llustration 5

Which type of isomerism is exhibit by following compound

$$\underset{(A)}{CH_3 - C \equiv N} \qquad \underset{(B)}{CH_3 - N \equiv C}$$

Solution

A and B exhibit functional isomerism.

Illustration 6

Give chain isomers in following compound

(A) n-Butane (B) 1-Butanal (C) 1-Butene

Solution

(A) $CH_3–CH_2–CH_2–CH_3$ (n-Butane) $(CH_3)_2CHCH_3$ (2-Methylpropane or Isobutane)

(B) $CH_3CH_2CH_2CH_2OH$ (1-Butanal) $(CH_3)_2CHCH_2OH$ (2-Methyl-1-butanol)

(C) $CH_3CH_2CH = CH_2$ (1-Butene) $(CH_3)_2C = CH_2$ (2-Methylpropene)

Illustration 7

Give position isomers of the following compounds

(A) 1-Butene (B) 1-Butyne

Solution

(A) $CH_3–CH_2 –C \equiv CH$ (1-Butyne) $CH_3C \equiv C – CH_3$ (2-Butyne)

(B) $CH_3–CH_2CH = CH_2$ (1-Butene) $CH_3CH = CH–CH_3$ (2-Butene)

➤ **Metamerism :** The compounds having same molecular formula but different number of carbon atoms (or alkyl groups) on either side of functional group, are called metamers.
e.g. ethers, thioethers, secondary amines, ketones, esters etc.

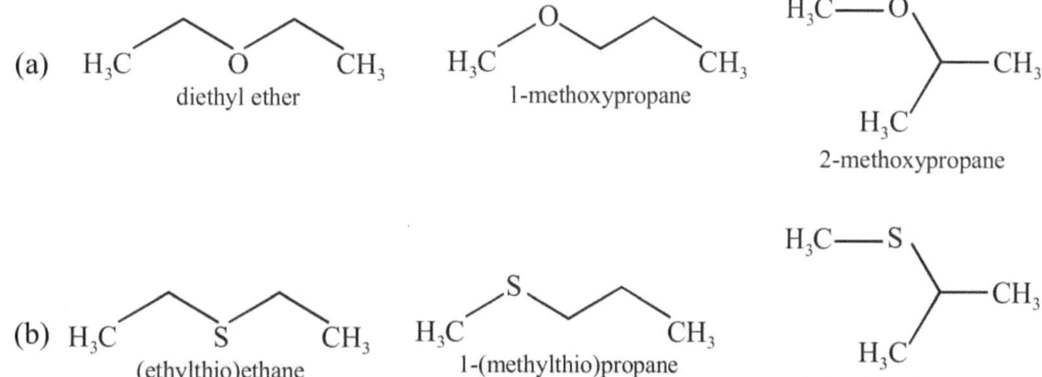

Illustration 8

Which type of isomerism is exhibited by following pair of compounds?

$$\underset{\text{N-Ethylethanamine}}{CH_3-CH_2-NH-CH_2-CH_3} \qquad \underset{\text{1-(N-Methyl) propanamine}}{CH_3-NH-CH_2-CH_2-CH_3}$$

Solution

Above pair of compounds represents metamerism.

- **Tautomerism :** This is a special type of functional isomerism in which the isomers differ in the arrangement of atoms but they exist in dynamic equilibrium with each other. For example, acetaldehyde and vinyl alcohol are tautomers.

```
   H  O                      OH
   |  ||                     |
H- C- C -H             H- C = C -H
   |                      |
   H                      H
Acetaldehyde          Vinyl alcohol
```

Tautomerism arises due to 1,3 migration of hydrogen atom from one polyvalent atom to other within the same molecules.

Knowledge Enhancer

Stereoisomerism was exhibit by compounds which have same structural formula and sequence of bonds but differ in the relative position of atoms or groups of atoms in space. It is majorly of two types

1. Geometrical Isomerism
2. Optical Isomerism

Geometrical Isomerism : also called cis trans isomerism is exhibited by alkanes because of the presence of double bond. This is due to the restricted rotation around carbon-carbon double bond. As a result, the position of the groups attached to these carbons is fixed in space. Here cis-isomer have identical group on either side whereas in trans-isomer identical groups are at opposite side of $C=C$.

```
A\       /A        A\       /B
   C = C              C = C
B/       \B        B/       \A
    cis                trans
```

Optical Isomerism is shown by substances which can rotate the plane of polarised light.

For example, this type of isomerism is shown by amino acid alanine.

Note : You will study about stereoisomerism in detail in higher classes.

4.9 TYPE OF ORGANIC REACTIONS (CHEMICAL PROPERTIES OF ORGANIC COMPOUND)

(1) COMBUSTION REACTION

The reaction in which substance (i.e. element or compound) burn with oxygen gas to form carbondioxide and water with release of a large amount of heat and light is called combustion. For example,

(i) $C + O_2 \longrightarrow CO_2$ + Heat and light

(ii) $CH_4 + O_2 \longrightarrow CO_2 + 2H_2O$ Heat and light

(iii) $CH_3—CH_2—OH + 3O_2 \longrightarrow 2CO_2 + 3H_2O$ + Heat and light

(iv) Combustion of ethylene $CH_2 = CH_2 + 3O_2 \longrightarrow 2CO_2 + 2H_2O$

Saturated hydrocarbons will generally burn in excess of air or oxygen with a blue flame but unsaturated hydrocarbons burn with a yellow flame with lots of black smoke.

This results sooty deposit on the metal plate. Sooty deposit is actually unburnt carbon which is produced due to incomplete combustion. The reason being that the carbon content of unsaturated compounds is more than the hydrogen content and hence carbon is not completely burnt and unburnt carbon deposits as a soot. In addition to that limiting supply of air result in incomplete combustion of even saturated hydrocarbon giving a sooty flame.

Fuel such as coal and petroleum have some amount of nitrogen and sulphur in them. Their combustion results in the formation of oxides of sulphur and nitrogen which are one major pollutants in the environment.

Some Examples of pollutant gases are SO_2, SO_3, NO, NO_2 etc.

Illustration 9

Observe the following experimental setup carefully

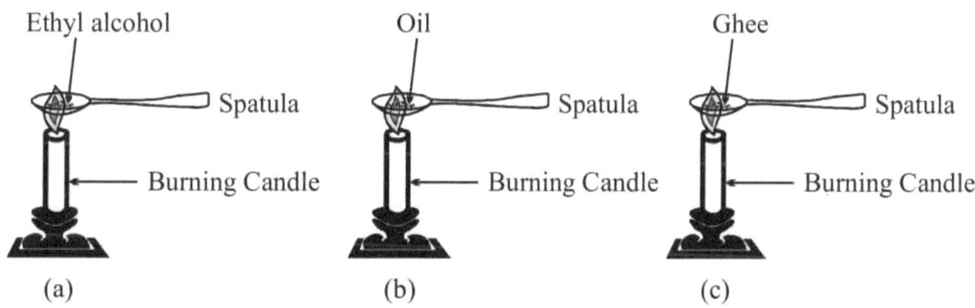

Which set up will produce smoke?

Solution :

Setup (b) will produce smoke as the oil taken in spoon contain unsaturated hydrocarbons which burns with luminous flame and produce more smoke.

Knowledge Enhancer

➤ **WHY DO SUBSTANCES BURN WITH OR WITHOUT A FALME?**

We have seen above that a candle or the LPG in the gas stove burns with a flame. However, we will observe the coal or charcoal in an '**angithi**' sometimes just glows red an gives out heat without a flame. This is because a flame is only produced when gaseous substances burn. When wood or charcoal is ignited, the volatile substances present vapourise and burn with a flame in the beginning.

A luminous flame is seen when the atoms of the gaseous substance are heated and start to glow. The colour produced by each element is a characteristic property of element. When we heat a copper wire in the flame of a gas stove and observe its colour. We can see that incomplete combustion gives soot which is carbon.

➤ **FORMATION OF COAL**

Coal and petroleum have been formed from biomass which has been subjected to various biological and geological processes. Coal is the remains of trees, ferns, or other plants that lived millions of years ago. These were crushed into the earth perhaps by earthquakes or volcanic eruptions. They were pressed down by layers of earth and rock. They slowly decayed into coal. The process of coal formation is known as carbonisation.

➤ **FORMATION OF PETROLEUM**

Oil and gases are the remains of million of tiny plants and animals that lived in the sea. When they died, their bodies sank in the sea bed and were covered by silt. Bacteria attacked the dead remains, forming them into oil and gas under the high pressures they were being subjected to. Meanwhile, the silt was slowly compressed into rock. The oil and gas seeped into the porous parts of the rock, and got trapped like water in a sponge.

---

(2) OXIDATION

Addition of oxygen to any substance or removal of hydrogen from any substance is called **oxidation**.

The substances which are capable of adding oxygen or removal of Hydrogen from other substance are called **oxidising agent**. Example:

Alkaline potassium permanganate and acidified potassium dichromate are good oxidising agents. These are easily oxidise alcohol to carboxylic acids.

$$\underset{\text{(Ethanol)}}{CH_3CH_2-OH} + 2[O] \xrightarrow[\text{or acidified } K_2Cr_2O_7+\Delta]{\text{Alkaline } KMnO_4+\Delta} \underset{\text{(Ethanoic acid)}}{CH_3-\overset{\overset{\displaystyle O}{\|}}{C}-OH} + H_2O$$

(3) ADDITION REACTION

Reactions in which a simple molecule added to an unsaturated compound to form a single product are called **addition reactions**.

Addition of Hydrogen gas:

Unsaturated hydrocarbons add hydrogen in presence of a catalyst such as Nickel, Platinum, or Palladium to form saturated hydrocarbons.

This process is called catalytic hydrogenation.

$$\underset{\text{(ethene)}}{H-\overset{H}{\overset{|}{C}}=\overset{H}{\overset{|}{C}}-H} + H-H \xrightarrow[Pt/\Delta]{\text{Ni or Pd}} \underset{\text{(ethane)}}{H-\underset{H}{\underset{|}{\overset{H}{\overset{|}{C}}}}-\underset{H}{\underset{|}{\overset{H}{\overset{|}{C}}}}-H}$$

$$\underset{\text{(ethyne)}}{H-C\equiv C-H} + 2H_2 \xrightarrow[\Delta]{Ni} \underset{\text{(ethane)}}{H-\underset{H}{\underset{|}{\overset{H}{\overset{|}{C}}}}-\underset{H}{\underset{|}{\overset{H}{\overset{|}{C}}}}-H}$$

Here Ni, Pd and Pt are catalysts and reducing agents which provide hydrogen to alkene and alkyne.

Test of unsaturated compound

The unsaturation means ($C=C$ or $C\equiv C$) present in organic compound can be tested by means of Baeyer's Reagent (1% alkaline $KMnO_4$) by observing the disappearance of colour pink ($KMnO_4$ Solution).

$$\underset{\text{(ethene)}}{CH_2=CH_2} + H_2O + [O] \xrightarrow{\text{Alkaline } KMnO_4} \underset{\text{(glycol)}}{\underset{OH}{\underset{|}{CH_2}}-\underset{OH}{\underset{|}{CH_2}}}$$

Application of Hydrogenation :- Hydrogenation (addition of H_2) is commonly used in the hydrogenation of vegetable oils (such as soyabean oil, cotton seed oil, groudnut oil etc.) in presence of Ni as catalyst to form fats (Vegetable oils generally have long unsaturated carbon chains while animal fats have saturated carbon chains).

$$\text{Vegetable oil (liquid)} + H_2 \xrightarrow{Ni/200^0C} \text{Vegetable Ghee (Solid)}$$

Animal fats generally contain saturated fatty acids which are said to be harmful for health.Therefore oils containing unsaturated fatty acids should be good for cooking.

Addition of halogen: (Cl_2, Br_2)

Halogen (Cl_2 and Br_2) can be added to unsaturated (C=C, C≡C) compound to form halogenated product.

$$>C=C< + X_2\ (Cl_2 \text{ or } Br_2) \xrightarrow{CCl_4} -\overset{X}{\overset{|}{\underset{|}{C}}}-\overset{X}{\overset{|}{\underset{|}{C}}}-$$

Application of Bromination: Bromination is used to test unsaturation (C = C or C ≡ C) present in the compound by observing the disappearance of red colour of Br_2 during reaction with an unsaturated Compound.

$$>C=C< + \underset{\text{(Red Colour)}}{Br_2} \xrightarrow{CCl_4} \underset{\text{(Colourless)}}{-\overset{|}{\underset{\underset{Br}{|}}{C}}-\overset{|}{\underset{\underset{Br}{|}}{C}}-}$$

(4) SUBSTITUTION REACTION

Reaction in which involves the direct replacement (displacement or substitution) of an atom or a group of atoms in an organic molecule by another atom or group of atoms without any change in the rest of the molecule are called **substitution reactions**.

$$R-X + Y \rightarrow R-Y + X$$

Halogenation of Alkane

Due to presence of strong carbon - carbon and carbon- Hydrogen bonds, saturated hydro carbons are quite less reactive and are inert to the cation of most of the reagents. Hence alkanes are also called paraffins (param means less, affinity means reactivity).

Alkanes react with halogen in presence of light

In presence of heat or light chlorine (F_2, Br_2 or I_2) reacts very rapidly with saturated hydrocarbons to form substitution products.

$$CH_4 + Cl_2 \xrightarrow[\text{on 520–670K}]{\text{Sunlight}} CH_3Cl + HCl$$

(Chloromethane substituted product)

with excess of chlorine all the hydrogen atoms of methane are replaced by one to form a number of products as shown below:

$$CH_3Cl + Cl_2 \xrightarrow{\text{Sunlight}} CH_2Cl_2 + HCl$$

(Dichloromethane)

$$CH_2Cl_2 + Cl_2 \xrightarrow{\text{Sunlight}} CHCl_3 + HCl$$

(Trichloro methane)

$$CHCl_3 + Cl_2 \xrightarrow{\text{Sunlight}} CCl_4 + HCl$$

(Carbon tetrachloride)

However with higher homologous of alkanes a number of product containing even one chlorine atom are formed.

$$CH_3-CH_2-CH_3 + Cl_2 \xrightarrow{\text{Sunlight}} CH_3-CH_2-CH_2-Cl + CH_3-\underset{}{\overset{Cl}{\overset{|}{C}}}H-CH_3$$

(Minor product) (Major Product) (due to stability of free radical)

(5) ELIMINATION REACTION

Reaction in which a simple molecule like HCl, H_2O, NH_3 etc. are removed from bigger molecule to form unsaturated compound is called **elimination reaction**.

$$R-\underset{|}{\overset{\overset{A}{|}}{C}}-\underset{|}{\overset{\overset{B}{|}}{C}}- \longrightarrow R-\underset{|}{C}=\underset{|}{C}- + AB$$

(reactant) (unsaturated product)

AB is eliminated during reaction.

Dehydration of alcohol :

Removal of water from alcohol is called **dehydration**. The substance which help in dehydration is known as dehydration agent (Conc. H_2SO_4, P_2O_5, Al_2O_3, etc)

$$R-\underset{|}{\overset{\overset{OH}{|}}{C}}-\underset{|}{\overset{\overset{H}{|}}{C}}- \xrightarrow[\Delta]{ConH_2SO_4} -\underset{|}{C}=\underset{|}{C}- + H_2O$$

(alkene)

$$CH_3-CH_2-OH \xrightarrow{Con.\ H_2SO_4} CH_2=CH_2 + H_2O$$

(Ethene Or Ethylene)

(6) REARRANGEMENT REACTION

Reaction in which bigger molecule rearrange to another different molecule without substitution, addition or ellimination is called **rearrangement reaction**.

The molecular formula of reactant and product remain same. In such reactions one compound converts into its isomer so such reactions are also known as **Isomerisation reaction**.

$$NH_4CNO \xrightarrow{\Delta} NH_2-\overset{\overset{O}{||}}{C}-NH_2$$

(Ammonium Cyanate) (Urea)

$$CH_3-CH_2-CH_2-CH_3 \xrightarrow[\Delta]{AlCl_3(\text{Catalyst})} CH_3-\underset{}{\overset{CH_3}{\overset{|}{C}H}}-CH_3$$

(Butane) 2-Methyl propane

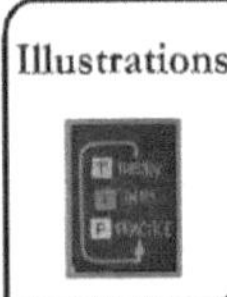

Illustration 10

Alkenes usually show which type of reaction?

Solution

Alkenes usually show addition reaction due to presence of unsaturation in the form of double bond.

Illustration 11

Give a test that can be used to differentiate chemically between butter and cooking oil?

Solution

Butter contains saturated fatty acids, whereas cooking oil contains unsaturated fatty acids. The unsaturation in a carbon compound can be tested with bromine solution.

Take a few drops of oil in a test tube. In another tube melt a little butter. Add a few drops of bromine water into both the test tubes and shake it well. The colour of bromine gets decolourized by cooking oil but remain unaffected by butter.

4.10 SOME IMPORTANT CARBON COMPOUNDS - ETHANOL AND ETHANOIC ACID

1. ETHANOL

▶ **PROPERTIES OF ETHANOL**

(i) Ethanol is a liquid at room temperature.

(ii) Ethanol is commonly called alcohol and is the active ingredient of all alcoholic drinks.

(iii) Ethanol is also soluble in water in all proportions.

▶ **REACTIONS OF ETHANOL**

(i) **Reaction with sodium :** Alcohols react with sodium leading to the evolution of hydrogen with ethanol and the by- product is sodium ethoxide.

$$2Na + 2CH_3CH_2OH \rightarrow 2CH_3CH_2O^-Na^+ + H_2$$

(Sodium ethoxide)

(ii) **Dehydration of Alcohol :** Heating ethanol at 443 K with excess of concentrated sulphuric acid results in the dehydration of ethanol to give ethene.

$$CH_3 - CH_2OH \xrightarrow[H_2SO_4]{\text{Hot conc.}} CH_2 = CH_2 + H_2O$$

The concentrated sulphuric acid can be regarded as a dehydrating agent which removes water from ethanol.

(iii) **Ester formation :** Under acid-catalyzed conditions, ethanol reacts with carboxylic acids to produce ethyl esters and water.

$$RCOOH + HOCH_2CH_3 \xrightarrow{H_3O^+} RCOOCH_2CH_3 + H_2O$$

(iv) **Oxidation :** Ethanol can be oxidized to acetaldehyde (also known as ethanal, is an organic chemical compound with the formula CH_3CHO, occurs naturally in ripe fruit, coffee, and fresh bread), and further oxidized to acetic acid. This oxidation is brought about by common oxidising agent used in organic chemistry like alkaline $KMnO_4$, acidified $K_2Cr_2O_7$, chromic acid etc.

$$CH_3CH_2OH \xrightarrow{\text{alk } KMnO_4} CH_3CHO \xrightarrow{\text{alk } KMnO_4} CH_3COOH$$

MANUFACTURE OF ETHANOL : (INDUSTRIAL SCALE)

Ethanol preparation from fermentation of sugar

Fermentation is a process whereby an organic compound is broken into smaller molecules by enzymes such as yeast. Ethanol is prepared by fermentaion of molasses. Molasses, a by product of sugar industry, has traces of sugar, which gets broken down into ethanol. The fermentation is initiated by yeast, which secretes two enzymes called invertase and zymase. These enzymes act as catalyst for converting sugar into ethanol. The reaction is exothermic and carbon dioxide is released in the process.

$$\underset{\text{Sucrose}}{C_{12}H_{22}O_{11}} + H_2O \xrightarrow{\text{Inverase}} \underset{\text{Glucose}}{C_6H_{12}O_6} + \underset{\text{Fructose}}{C_6H_{12}O_6}$$

$$\underset{\text{Glucose or fructose}}{C_6H_{12}O_6} \xrightarrow{\text{Zymase}} \underset{\text{Ethanol}}{2C_2H_5OH} + 2CO_2$$

Molasses is heated to about 20 to 30°C in an airtight container. Yeast is mixed in the molasses. The airtight container has outlets for removal of carbon dioxide released during the fermentation process. Ethanol and water vapours that are formed are collected and separated by fractional distillation.

HOW DO ALCOHOLS AFFECT LIVING BEINGS?

(i) When large quantities of ethanol are consumed, it tends to slow metabolic processes and to depress the central nervous system. This results in lack of coordination, mental confusion, drowsiness, lowering of the normal inhibitions, and finally stupor.

(ii) The individual may feel relaxed but does not realise that his sense of judgement, sense of timing, and muscular coordination have been seriously impaired.

(iii) Intake of methanol in very small quantities can cause death. Methanol is oxidised to methanal in the liver. Methanal reacts rapidly with the components of cells. It causes the protoplasm to get coagulated, in much the same way an egg is coagulated by cooking.

(iv) Methanol also affects the optic nerve, causing blindness. Ethanol is an important industrial solvent. To prevent the misuse of ethanol produced for industrial use, it is made unfit for drinking by adding poisonous substances like methanol dyes are also added to colour the alcohol blue so that it can be identified easily. This is called **denatured alcohol**.

(v) Consumption of small quantities of dilute ethanol causes drunkenness. Even though this practice is condemned, it is a socially widespread practice. However, intake of even a small quantity of pure ethanol (called absolute alcohol) can be lethal. Also, long-term consumption of alcohol leads to many health problems.

Ethanol is a good solvent. It is also used in medicines such as tincture of iodine, cough syrups, and many tonics.

ALCOHOL AS A FUEL

Sugarcane plants are one of the most efficient convertors of sunlight into chemical energy. Sugarcane juice can be used to prepare molasses which is fermented to give alcohol (ethanol). Some countries now use alcohol as an additive in petrol.

It is a cleaner fuel which gives rise to only carbon dioxide and water on burning in sufficient air (oxygen). It is known as Power alcohol.

USES OF ETHANOL :

(i) Ethanol is used for manufacturing of paints, dyes, varnishes.

(ii) Ethanol is used in medicines especially for disinfecting area on the skin before giving an injection.It is used for sterilization of syringes in hospitals.

(iii) Ethanol is used for preparation of compounds such as chloroform and ether.

(iv) Ethanol is used for making thermometer that is used for measuring low temperature.

(v) Ethanol is used in spirit lamps.

(vi) Ethanol blended fuel called rectified spirit is used as a substitute for fuels in vehicles that are environmental pollutant. They give off low emissions of carbon monoxide gas that is harmful to the environment. Ethanol is the main component of alcoholic beverages such as rum, whisky and beer.

2. ETHANOIC ACID

▶ PROPERTIES OF ETHANOIC ACID :

Ethanoic acid is commonly called acetic acid and belongs to carboxylic acid group.

5-8% solution of acetic acid in water is called vinegar and is used widely as a preservative in pickles.

The melting point of pure ethanoic acid is 290 K and hence it often freezes during winter in cold climates. This gave rise to its name glacial acetic acid.

The group carboxylic acids are obviously characterised by a special acidity.

However, unlike mineral acids like HCl, which are completely ionised, carboxylic acids are weak acids because they do not ionised completely.

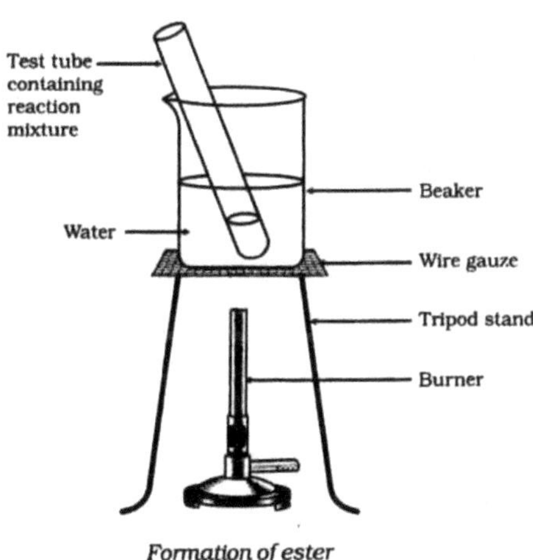

Formation of ester

▶ PHYSICAL PROPERTIES :

(i) Ethanoic acid is a colouless liquid with sour taste and typical vinegar smell.

(ii) It is miscible with water in all proportions.

(iii) The acid boils at 391 K (118°C).

(iv) On cooling, pure ethanoic acid freezes to form ice like flakes. They look like a glacial. Due to this property, pure ethanoic acid is often called glacial ehtanoic acid or glacial acetic acid.

Pure, water-free acetic acid (glacial acetic acid) is a colourless liquid that attracts water from the environment (hygroscopy), and freezes below 16.7°C (62°F) to a colouless crystalline solid. Acetic acid is one of the simplest carboxylic acids (the second-simplest, next to formic acid). Acetic acid is corrosive, and its vapour causes irritation to the eyes, dry and burning nose, sore throat and congestion to the lungs.

▶ CHEMICAL PROPERTIES :

The hydrogen (H) atom in the carboxyl group (–COOH) in carboxylic acids such as acetic acid can be given off as an H^+ ion (proton), giving them their acidic character. Acetic acid is a weak, effectively monoprotic acid in aqueous solution. Acetic acid is corrosive to metals including iron, magnesium and zinc forming hydrogen gas and metal salts called acetates.

▶ REACTIONS OF ETHANOIC ACID

(i) Esterification reaction: Esters are most commonly formed by reaction of an acid and an alcohol. Ethanoic acid reacts with absolute ethanol in the presence of an acid catalyst to give an ester -

$$\underset{\text{(Ethanoic acid)}}{CH_3COOH} + \underset{\text{(Ethanol)}}{CH_3 - CH_2OH} \xrightarrow{H_2SO_4} \underset{\text{(Ester - Ethyl ethanoate)}}{H_3C-\underset{\underset{O}{\|}}{C}-O-CH_2-CH_3} + H_2O$$

Uses of Ester :

(i) Esters are sweet-smelling substances. These are used in making perfumes and flavouring agents.

(ii) Esters react in the presence of an acid or a base to give back the alcohol and carboxylic acid. This reaction is known as **saponification** because it is used in the preparation of soap.

$$CH_3COOC_2H_5 \xrightarrow{NaOH} C_2H_5OH + CH_3COONa$$

(ii) Reaction with a base: Like mineral acids, ethanoic acid reacts with a base such as sodium hydroxide to give a salt (sodium ethanoate is commonly called sodium acetate) and water and heat is evolved.

$$NaOH + CH_3COOH \rightarrow CH_3COONa + H_2O$$

(iii) Reaction with carbonates and hydrogencarbonates: Ethanoic acid reacts with carbonates and hydrogencarbonates to give a salt, carbon dioxide and water. The salt producing is commonly called sodium acetate.

$$2CH_3COOH + Na_2CO_3 \rightarrow 2CH_3COONa + H_2O + CO_2\uparrow$$
$$CH_3COOH + NaHCO_3 \rightarrow CH_3COONa + H_2O + CO_2\uparrow$$

▶ **USES :** Ethanoic acid or acetic acid is used :

(i) as a solvent in industry as well as in laboratory.
(ii) for making dyes, perfumes and medicines.
(iii) for making synthetic vinegar.
(iv) for making basic copper acetate $[Cu(CH_3COO)_2 . Cu(OH)_2]$ which is used in green paints.
(v) for making aluminium acetate $[(CH_3COO)_3 Al]$ used in preparing water proof fabrics.
(vi) as a laboratory reagent for carrying chemical reactions.

It is an important chemical reagent and industrial chemical that is used in the production of polyethylene terephthalate mainly used in soft drink bottles; cellulose acetate, mainly for photographic film; and polyvinyl acetate for wood glue, as well as synthetic fibres and fabrics. In households diluted acetic acid is often used in descaling agents. In the food industry acetic acid is used under the food additive code E260 as an acidity regulator.

4.11 SOAPS AND DETERGENTS :

Soaps are sodium or potassium fatty acids salts, produced from the alkaline hydrolysis of fats (higher fatty acids) in a chemical reaction called saponification. They are of biological origin. Each soap molecule has a long hydrocarbon chain, sometimes called its 'tail', with a carboxylate 'head'. In water, the sodium or potassium ions float free, leaving a negatively-charged head.

$$\begin{array}{l} CH_2-O-COC_{17}H_{35} \\ | \\ CH-O-COC_{17}H_{35} + 3NaOH \\ | \\ CH_2-O-COC_{17}H_{35} \\ \text{Glyceride} \end{array} \longrightarrow \begin{array}{l} CH_2OH \\ | \\ CHOH + \underset{\text{Soap}}{3C_{17}H_{35}COO^-Na^+} \\ | \\ CH_2OH \\ \text{Glycerol} \end{array}$$

Before dealing with cleaning action or soap let as understand few points:

- The salts or fatty acids have an ionic polar head group, the carboxylate and a long non-polar hydrocarbon chain.

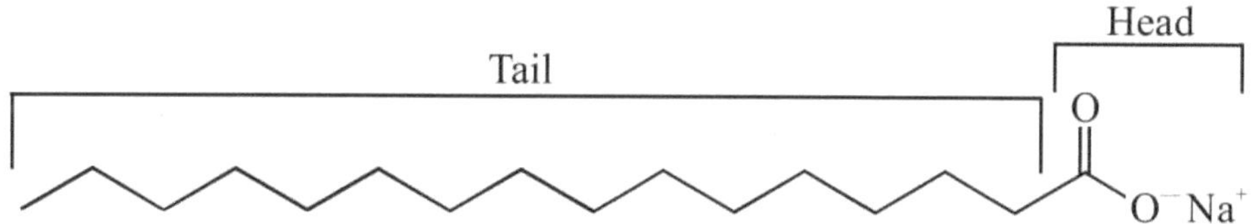

- The polar group is hydrophilic (i.e. water-loving), the non-polar portion is hydrophobic (i.e. water-hating) or liophilic.
- As a result aqueous solutions of this type of compound tend to form ordered aggregatcs such as micelles and bilayers.
- Here the polar groups are exposed to the water and the hydrocarbon portions are "buried" within the core, away from the water.

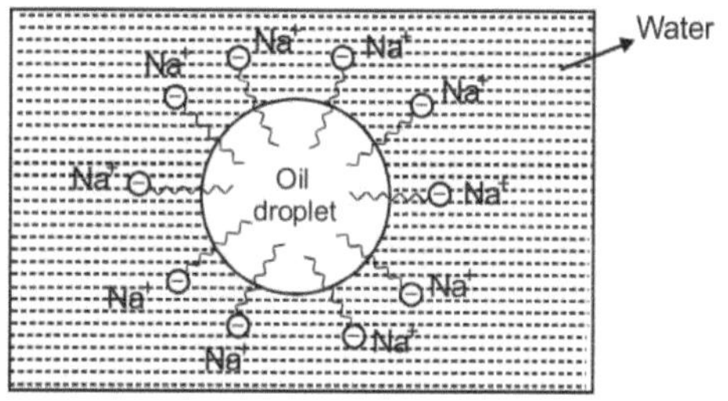

Use of sodium salt of long chain carboxylic acids (Soap) as cleaning agent

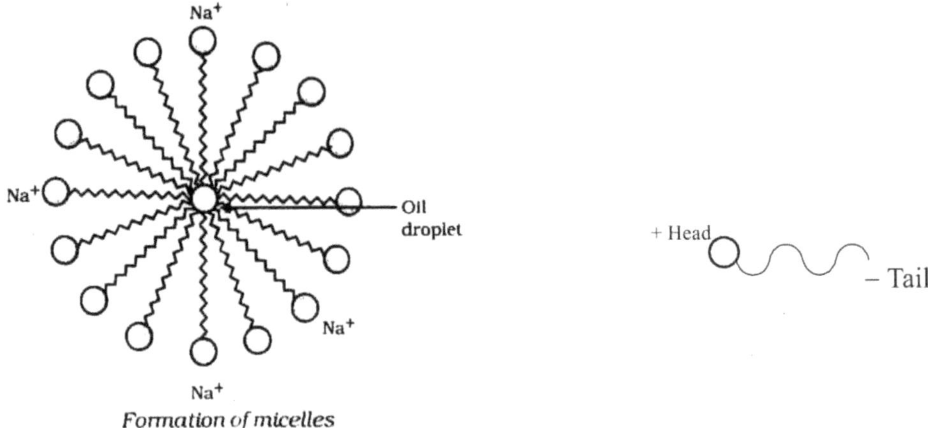

Formation of micelles

This Activity demonstrates the effect of soap in cleaning. Most dirt is oily in nature and as we know, oil does not dissolve in water. The molecules of soap are sodium or potassium salts of long-chain carboxylic acids. The ionic-end of soap dissolves in water while the carbon chain dissolves in oil. The soap molecules, thus form structures called micelles where one end of the molecules is towards the oil droplet while the ionic-end faces outside. This forms an emulsion in water. When we rub the cloth dirt particles with micelle leave the surface of cloth and it become clean thus the soap micelle thus helps in dissolving the dirt in water and we can wash our clothes clean.

MICELLES :

Soaps are molecules in which the two ends have differing properties, one is hydrophilic, that is, it dissolves in water, while the other end is hydrophobic, that is, it dissolves in hydrocarbons.

When soap is at the surface of water, the hydrophobic 'tail' of soap will not be soluble in water and the soap will align along the surface of water with the ionic end in water and the hydrocarbon 'tail' protruding out of water.

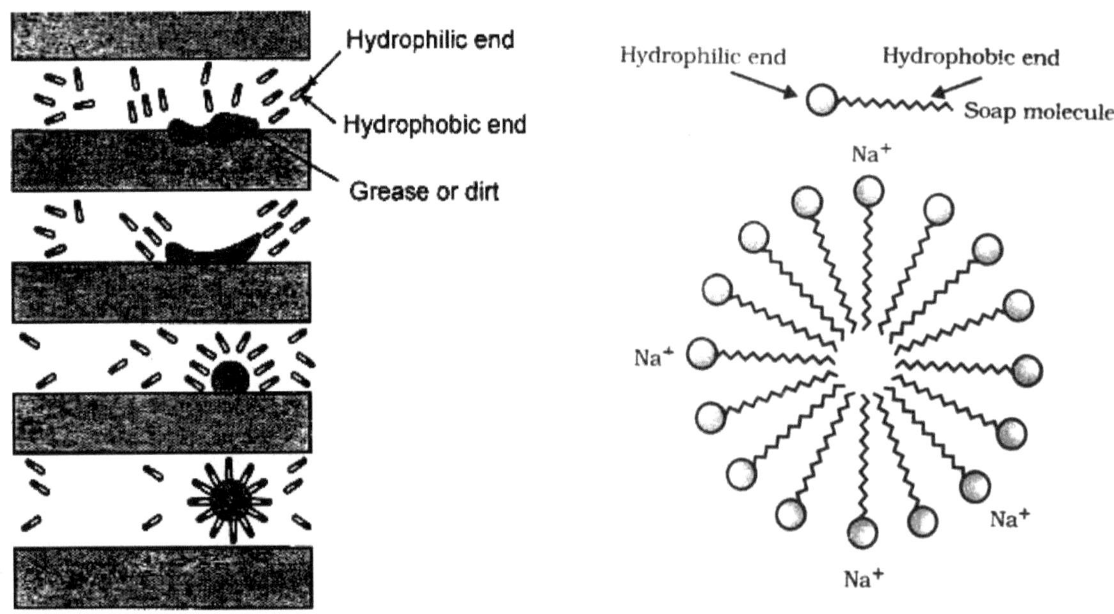

EFFECT OF SOAP IN CLEANING

Inside water, these molecules have a unique orientation that keeps the hydrocarbon portion out of the water. This is achieved by forming clusters of molecules in which the hydrophobic tails are in the interior of the cluster and the ionic ends are on the surface of the cluster. This formation is called a micelle. Soap in the form of a micelle is able to clean, since the oily dirt will be collected in the centre of the micelle. The micelles stay in solution as a colloid and will not come together to precipitate because of ion-ion repulsion. Thus, the dirt suspended in the micelles is also easily rinsed away. The soap micelles are large enough to scatter light. Hence a soap solution appears cloudy.

DETERGENT

Have you ever observed while bathing that foam is formed with difficulty and an insoluble substance (scum) remains after washing with water? This is caused by the reaction of soap with the calcium and magnesium salts, which cause the hardness of water. Hence you need to use a larger amount of soap. This problem is overcome by using another class of compounds called detergents as cleansing agents. Detergents are generally ammonium or sulphonate salts of long chain carboxylic acids. The charged ends of these compounds do not form insoluble precipitates with the calcium and magnesium ions in hard water. Thus, they remain effective in hard water. Detergents are usually used to make shampoos and products for cleaning clothes.

Illustrations

Illustration 12

Which gas is evolved during the process of fermentation?

Solution

Carbon dioxide gas is evolved during fermentation.

Illustration 13

Explain the formation of scum when hard water is treated with soap.

Solution

When soap solution is added into a sample of hard water, scum is formed. This is due to the formation of calcium or magnesium salts of the fatty acids.

$$RCOONa + Ca^{2+} \rightarrow (RCOO)_2Ca \downarrow + Na^+$$

(soap present in hard water) scum as precipitate

4.12 SOME IMPORTANT ORGANIC COMPOUNDS

1. **CHLORO - FLUORO CARBON OR FREONS**

When carbon atom forms compound with chlorine and fluorine, to complete its valencies, then it is known as choro-fiuoro carbon or freons.

OR

Polychloro-Fluoro derivatives of alkanes are known as chloro-Fluoro carbon or freons.

For nomenclature of freons the number of carbon, hydrogen and fluorine atoms are considered.
Example - Freon XYZ

where X = No. of carbon atom present in freon molecule-1

Y = No. of hydrogen atoms + 1

Z = No. of fluorine atoms.

Molecular formula	X	Y	Z	Name
$CFCl_3$	0	1	1	Freon – 11
CF_2Cl_2	0	1	2	Freon – 12
$C_2F_2Cl_4$	1	1	2	Freon – 112
$C_2F_3Cl_3$	1	1	3	Freon – 113
$C_2F_4Cl_2$	1	1	4	Freon – 114

Uses :

(i) Used as refrigerant in refrigerators, air conditioners and cold storage.

(ii) Used as inert solvent.

Note: CFC's are harmful for ozone layer so now many countries have baned its use as freezing agent.

2. POLYMERS

Polymers are compounds of high molecular weight which is formed by combination of one or more molecules of lower molecular weight. In nature many polymer compound like rubber. starch, cellulose are found which are very important in our daily life . In addition to these many ; polymers are formed artificially, they are known as synthetic polymer i.e. synthetic fibres, artificial rubber plastic, resin etc.

3. ARTIFICAL FIBRES

(A) Nylon 66: It is formed by condensation of units of adipic acid (6 carbon atom) and hexa methylene diamine (6 carbon atom) so it is known as Nylon 66.

Due to presence of amide bond this polymer is known as polyamide polymer.

$$\underset{\text{Adipic acid}}{nHOOC-(CH_2)_4-COOH} + \underset{\text{Hexa methylene diamine}}{nNH_2-(CH_2)_6-NH_2} \rightarrow$$

$$\underset{\substack{\text{Nylon 66} \\ \text{(Polyamide polymer)}}}{[-CO-(CH_2)_4-CO-NH-(CH_2)_6-NH-]_n} + nH_2O$$

Melting point of nylon is high therefore its fibres have high tensile strength, they are insoluble in many solvents.

Uses :

(i) Used for manufacturing of tyres, clothes fibres, ropes brushes etc.

(ii) For manufacturing of gears and bearings in machine.

(B) **Rayon** : It is regenerated cellulose, to manufacture rough paper (cellulose) is washed with sodium hydroxide, after that it is dissolved in carbon disulphide (CS_2) to obtain solution of cellulose. The solution is passed through fine holes in dilute sulphuric acid by which fine shinny rayon fibres are formed

Uses: Used for manufacturing of clothes, threads and carpets etc.

4. PLASTICS

Generally plastic are those substances which is be remolded into various desired shape. Some important plastic polymer are as follows.

(i) **Polyethene:** Ethene, in the presence of catalyst, at high temprature and pressure polymeries to form polyethylene.

This is flexible and hard plastic.

$$\underset{\text{Ethene}}{n\,(CH_2 = CH_2)} \rightarrow \underset{\text{polyethylene}}{(\!-CH_2 - CH_2-\!)_n}$$

Uses: Used in manufacture of polyethylene bags, mould material, pipes, tubes, bottles etc.

(ii) **Polyvinyl chloride (PVC):** It is obtained by the polymerisation of vinyl chloride.

$$\underset{\text{Vinyl Chloride}}{n\,(CH_2 = \underset{\substack{|\\Cl}}{CH})} \xrightarrow{\text{Polymerisation}} \underset{\text{P.V.C.}}{[-CH_2 - \underset{\substack{|\\Cl}}{CH} -]_n}$$

Uses: P.V.C. is used in the manufacturing of rain coats, bags, shoes, sleepers, hospital bed sheets, toys pipes, insulation layers, phonogram records etc.

(iii) **Orlon:** It is prepared from vinyl cyanide. It is also known as poly vinyl cyanide or poly acrylonitrile (PAN.) or orlon

$$n\left(CH_2 = \underset{\substack{|\\CN}}{CH}\right) \rightarrow \left[-CH_2 - \underset{\substack{|\\CN}}{CH} - CH_2 - \underset{\substack{|\\CN}}{CH}-\right]_n$$

Vinyl cyanide or acrylonitrile (ORLON)

Uses: It is used in manufacturing of woolen sweaters, bathing suits,wool like fibre which forms beds and pillows.

(iv) **Polymethyl methacrylate:** It is prepared by the polymerisation of methyl methacrylate.

$$nCH_2 = \underset{\substack{|\\CH_3}}{C} — COOCH_3 \rightarrow \left[-CH_2 - \overset{\substack{COOCH_3\\|}}{\underset{\substack{|\\CH_3}}{C}} -\right]$$

Methyl methacrylate Polymethyl methacrylate (P.M.MA.)

It is hard and transparent, it is used for making covers of car lights and attractive sign boards.

Uses: Used as lenses, ventilators and glasses for aircraft windows.

(v) **Polystyrene:** It is obtained by the polymerisation of styrene.

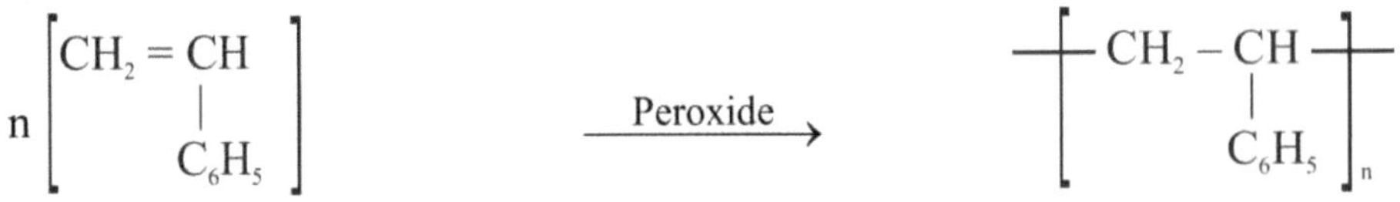

$$n\begin{bmatrix} CH_2 = CH \\ \quad\;\; | \\ \quad\;\; C_6H_5 \end{bmatrix} \xrightarrow{\text{Peroxide}} \left[\begin{matrix} -CH_2 - CH- \\ \quad\quad\;\; | \\ \quad\quad\;\; C_6H_5 \end{matrix} \right]_n$$

Styrene Polystyrene

Uses: Used for making bottle corks, small radio cabinets, spare parts of refrigerators, combs, toys, ceramic tiles, cups and **packing materials.**

5. SYNTHETIC RUBBER

Natural rubber is obtained as liquid form which is known as rubber latex. It is polymer of isoprene.

$$\begin{bmatrix} CH_2 = CH - C = CH_2 \\ \quad\quad\quad\quad\;\; | \\ \quad\quad\quad\quad\;\; CH_3 \end{bmatrix} \rightarrow \begin{bmatrix} -CH_2 - CH = C - CH_2- \\ \quad\quad\quad\quad\quad\;\; | \\ \quad\quad\quad\quad\quad\;\; CH_3 \end{bmatrix}_n$$

Isoprene Natural rubber

In latex acetic acid is mixed to convert it into solid thus the rubber obtained, does not used to form refined products because it is high elastic and it has low tensile strength.
To increase the effciency and tensile strength, it is mixed and heated with sulphur. This process is known as **Vulcanisation**. The rubber so obtained, is hard, not elastic and resistant to abrassion.
Uses: Rubber is used in manufacturing of tyres and tubes.

During first world war when supply of natural rubber to Germany was banned then scientist tried to discover new sources of rubber and they obtained rubber like substance by the polymerisation of 2, 3 dimethyl 1, 3- butadiene.
For this, 2. 3 dimethyl 1,3 butadiene is exposed to atmosphere of CO_2 and catalyse by sodium to form rubber like substance which is named as BUNA.
which indicates Bu = Butadiene
Na = sodium catalyst
From industrial point of view many synthetic rubber are formed such as

(i) BUNA - S (formed from polymerisation of butadiene and ethylene or styrene)

(ii) BUNA - N (formed from polymerisation of butadiene and nitrile)

Uses : Synthetic rubber is used for the manufacturing of house pipes, oil canes, tyres, tubes, medical equipments, shoe soal etc Neoprene rubber is hard so it is used to manufacture gaskets.

POINTS TO REMEMBER

1. Carbon forms a large variety of compounds because of its tetravalency and the property of catenation.
2. Hydrocarbons are the compounds of carbon and hydrogen.
3. Hydrocarbons are of two types - saturated hydrocarbons (alkanes) and unsaturated hydrocarbons (alkenes and alkynes).
4. Carbon forms covalent bonds with itself and other elements such as hydrogen, oxygen, sulphur, nitrogen and chlorine.
5. The functional groups such as alcohols, aldehydes, ketones and carboxylic acids show characteristic properties to the carbon compounds that contain them.
6. A group/series of hydrocarbons having similar structure and similar properties (i.e.same functional group) is called a homologous series.
7. Carbon chains may be in the form of straight chains, branched chains or rings.
8. Carbon compounds with identical molecular formula but different structures are called structural isomers.
9. Saturated hydrocarbons on combustion give carbondioxide and water with lots of heat.
10. Unsaturated hydrocarbons undergo addition reactions while saturated hydrocarbons undergo substitution reactions.
11. Ethanol and Ethanoic acid (glacial acetic acid) are carbon compounds of importance in our daily life.
12. The molecules of soap are sodium or potassium salts of long chain carboxylic acids.
13. The action of soaps and detergents is based on the presence of both hydrophobic and hydrophilic groups in the molecule and this helps to emulsify the oily dirt and hence its removal.
14. Covalent bond: A covalent bond is a bond formed by sharing of electrons between atoms. In a covalent bond, the shared pair of electrons belongs to the valence shell of both the atoms.
15. Properties of covalent compounds:
    (a) Physical states: They are generally liquids or gases. Some covalent compounds may exist as solids.
    (b) Solubility: They are generally insoluble in water and other polar solvents but soluble in organic solvents like benzene, toluene etc.
    (c) Melting and boiling point: They generally have low melting and boiling points.
    (d) Electrical conductivity: They do not conduct electrical current.
16. Carbon forms covalent bonds.
17. Electronegativity - It is the ability of an atom to attract a shared pair of electrons towards itself.
18. If the atoms forming a covalent bond have different electronegativities, the atom with higher electronegativity pulls the shared pair of electron towards itself. Thus, the atom with the higher electronegativity develops a partial negative charge and the atom with the lower electronegativity develops a partial positive charge. This covalent bond with some polarity is called polar covalent bond.
19. Carbon forms a large number of compounds because of two unique properties:
    (a) Tetravalency (b) Catenation

20. Tetravalency of carbon:

Atomic number = 6 ; Electronic configuration: 2, 4

Valence electrons = 4; Valency = 4

So, carbon needs four electrons to attain noble gas configuration. Or in other words, carbon has the ability to form four bonds with carbon or atoms of other mono-valent elements.

21. Catenation: Carbon has the unique ability to form bonds with other atoms of carbon, giving rise to large molecules. This property is called catenation.

22. Classification of hydrocarbons:

(a) Aliphatic or open chain hydrocarbons: These are the carbon compounds which have carbon carbon long open chains. They are classified as:

(i) Saturated hydrocarbons: These hydrocarbons have all carbon - carbon single bonds.

(ii) Unsaturated hydrocarbons: These hydrocarbons have at least one carbon - carbon double or triple bonds.

- Hydrocarbons with at least one carbon-carbon double bond are called alkenes.
- General formula = C_nH_{2n} where n = number of carbon atoms.
- Hydrocarbons with at least one carbon-carbon triple bond are called alkynes.
- General formula = C_nH_{2n-2} where n = number of carbon atoms

(b) Cyclic or closed chain hydrocarbons: These are the hydrocarbons which have carbon carbon closed chain.

They are classified as:

(i) Alicyclic hydrocarbons: These are the hydrocarbons which do not have aromatic benzene ring in their structure.

(ii) Aromatic hydrocarbons: These are the hydrocarbons which have benzene ring in their structure. When hydrogen bonded to carbon of benzene is substituted with halogens, radicals or other functional groups, the derivatives are called aromatic compounds.

23. Benzene: It is an aromatic hydrocarbon which has the molecular formula C_6H_6. It has alternating carbon - carbon single and double bonds.

24. Conditions for Isomerism:

(a) Only alkanes with more than three carbon atoms can have isomers.

(b) The side chains cannot be present on the terminal carbons.

25. Homologous Series: A series of organic compounds in which every succeeding member differs from the previous one by $-CH_2$ or 14 u. The molecular formula of all the members of a homologous series can be derived from a general formula.

26. Properties of a homologous series: As the molecular mass increases in a series, so physical properties of the compounds show a variation, but chemical properties which are determined by a functional group remain the same within a series.

27. Homologous series of alkanes: General formula: C_nH_{2n+2} where n = number of carbon atoms.

28. Homologous series of alkenes: General formula: C_nH_{2n} where n = number of carbon atoms.

29. Homologous series of alkynes: General formula: = C_nH_{2n-2} where n = number of carbon atoms.

30. Functional group: An atom or a group of atoms which when present in a compound gives specific properties to it, regardless of the length and nature of the carbon chain is called functional group.

31. Catalysts are substances that cause a reaction to occur or proceed at a different rate without the reaction being affected.

32. Oxidizing agents are substances which are capable of providing oxygen to other compounds for their axidation. Example: Alkaline $KMnO_4$, acidified $K_2Cr_2O_7$ etc.

33. Soaps are sodium or potassium salts of long chain carboxylic acids.

34. Structure of soap molecule: The structure of soap molecule consists of a long hydrocarbon tail at one end which is hydrophobic in nature. The other end is the ionic part which is hydrophilic in nature.

35. Cleansing action of soap: When soap is at the surface of water, the ionic end of soap orients itself towards water and the hydrocarbon 'tail' orients itself towards the dirt. Thus, clusters of molecules are formed in which the hydrophobic tails are in the interior of the cluster and the ionic ends are on the surface of the cluster. The formation of cluster is called micelle.

    Soap in the form of a micelle is able to clean, since the oily dirt will be collected in the centre of the micelle. The micelles stay in solution as a colloid and will not come together to precipitate because of ion-ion repulsion. Now, when water is agitated, the dirt suspended in the micelles is also easily rinsed away.

36. When hard water is treated with soap, scum is formed. This is caused by the reaction of soap with the calcium and magnesium salts, which cause the hardness of water.

37. Detergents are generally ammonium or sulphonate salts of long chain carboxylic acids.

38. Detergents do not form scum with hard water. This is because the charged ends of these compounds do not form insoluble precipitates with the calcium and magnesium ions in hard water. Thus, they remain effective in hard water.

CONCEPT APPLICATION LEVEL - I [NCERT Questions]

Q.1 What would be the electron dot structure of carbon dioxide which has the formula CO_2?

Ans. The electron dot formula of CO_2 is given below:

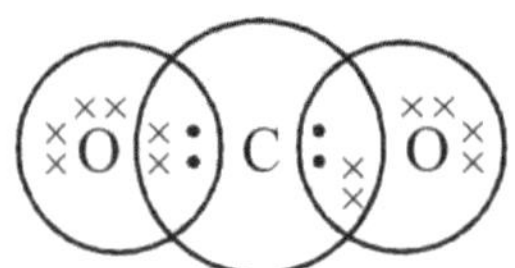

Q.2 What would be the electron dot structure of a molecule of sulphur which is made up of eight atoms of sulphur? [Hint: The eight atoms of suphur are joined together in the form of a ring.]

Ans. The electron dot structure of a molecule of sulphur which is made of eight atoms of suphur is given below: Electron-dot structure of sulphur molecule, S_8.

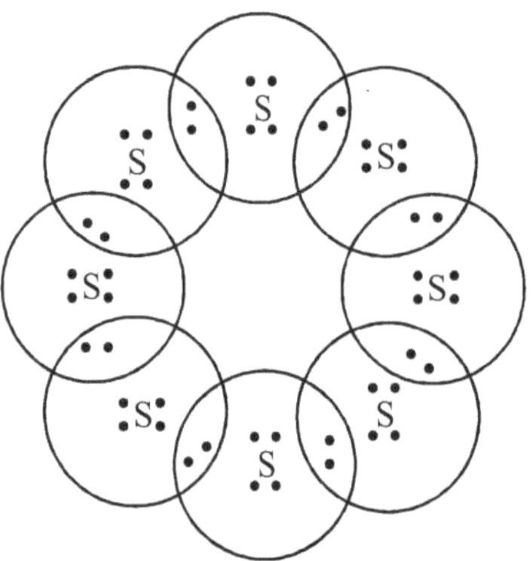

Ring structure of S_8 molecule

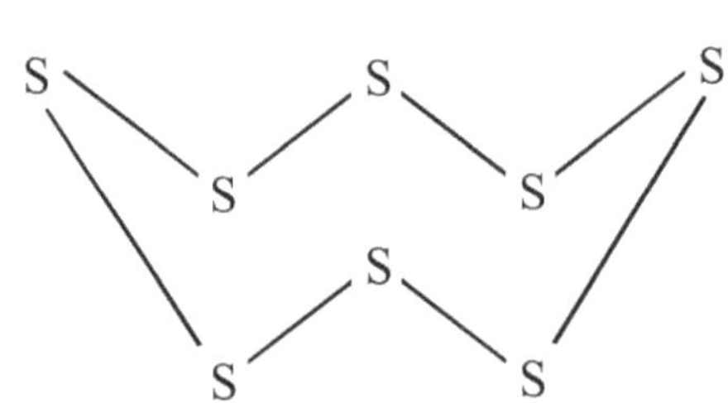

Crown Shape of S_8 molecule

Q.3 How many structural isomers can you draw for pentane?

Ans. Three structural isomers can be drawn for pentane:

$$\begin{array}{ccccccccccc} & & H & & H & & H & & H & & H \\ & & | & & | & & | & & | & & | \\ H & - & C & - & C & - & C & - & C & - & C & - H \\ & & | & & | & & | & & | & & | \\ & & H & & H & & H & & H & & H \end{array} \quad \text{or} \quad (\overset{1}{C}H_3-\overset{2}{C}H_2-\overset{3}{C}H_2-\overset{4}{C}H_2-\overset{5}{C}H_3)$$

Pentane

$$H_3\overset{1}{C}-\underset{\underset{CH_3}{|}}{\overset{2}{C}H}-\overset{3}{C}H_2-\overset{4}{C}H_3;$$

2–Methyl butane

$$H_3C-\underset{\underset{CH_3}{|}}{\overset{\overset{CH_3}{|}}{C}}-CH_3$$

2,2–dimethyl propane

Q.4 What are the two properties of carbon which lead to the huge number of carbon compounds we see around us?

Ans. The two properties of carbon are its tetra covalency and the catenation which lead to huge number of carbon compounds we see around us.

Q.5 What will be the formula and electron dot structure of cyclopentane?

Ans. The formula of cyclopentane will be C_5H_{10}. Its electron dot structure will be as shown below

```
        H  H                         H H
     H   C        H                   \/
 H××C        C··×H                H\  C   /H
 H×.               ·×H            H/C     C\H
    C  ··   C                      H\|    |/H
 H×           ×H                   H/C —— C\H
```

or

Q.6 Draw the structures for the following compounds: (i) Ethanoic acid (ii) Bromopentane (iii) Butanone (iv) Hexanal. Are structural isomers possible for bromopentane?

Ans. The structure of the compounds are

(i) Ethanoic acid

```
   H  O
   |  ||
H–C–C–OH
   |
   H
```

(ii) Bromopentane

```
   H  H  H  H  H
   |  |  |  |  |
H–C–C–C–C–C–Br
   |  |  |  |  |
   H  H  H  H  H
```

(iii) Butanone

```
   H  O  H  H
   |  ||  |  |
H–C–C–C–C–H
   |      |  |
   H      H  H
```

(iv) Hexanal

```
   H  H  H  H  H  O
   |  |  |  |  |  ||
H–C–C–C–C–C–C–H
   |  |  |  |  |
   H  H  H  H  H
```

Bromopentane has a chain of five carbon atoms. It can exist in a number of forms which are structural isomers.

(i) $\overset{5}{H_3C}-\overset{4}{C}H_2-\overset{3}{C}H_2-\overset{2}{C}H_2-\overset{1}{C}H_2-Br$

1–Bromopentane

(ii) $\overset{5}{H_3C}-\overset{4}{C}H_2-\overset{3}{C}H_2-\overset{2}{C}H(Br)-\overset{1}{C}H_3$

2–Bromopentane

(iii) $\overset{5}{H_3C}-\overset{4}{C}H_2-\overset{3}{C}H(Br)-\overset{2}{C}H_2-\overset{1}{C}H_3$

3–Bromopentane

(iv) $\overset{4}{H_3C}-\overset{3}{C}H(CH_3)-\overset{2}{C}H_2-\overset{1}{C}H_2-Br$

1-Bromo-3-methylbutane

(v) $\overset{4}{C}H_3-\overset{3}{C}H_2-\overset{2}{C}H(CH_3)-\overset{1}{C}H_2-Br$

1-Bromo-2-methylbutane

(vi) $\overset{3}{C}H_3-\overset{2}{C}(CH_3)_2-\overset{1}{C}H_2-Br$

1–Bromo–2,2–dimethylpropane

Q.7 How would you name the following compounds?

Ans. (i) CH_3-CH_2-Br
Bromoethane

(ii)
$$\begin{array}{c} H \\ | \\ H-C=O \end{array}$$
Methanal

(iii)
$$\begin{array}{cccccccccc} & H & & H & & H & & H & & \\ & | & & | & & | & & | & & \\ H- & C & - & C & - & C & - & C & - & C\equiv C-H \\ & | & & | & & | & & | & & \\ & H & & H & & H & & H & & \end{array}$$
1–Hexyne or Hex–1–yne

Q.8 Why is the conversion of ethanol to ethanoic acid an oxidation reaction?

Ans. The conversion of ethanol (CH_3CH_2OH) to ethanoic acid (CH_3COOH) is called an oxidation reaction because oxygen is added to it during this conversion.

$$\underset{\text{Ethanol}}{CH_3CH_2OH} + \underset{\text{Nascent oxygen}}{2[O]} \xrightarrow[\text{Heat}]{\text{Alkaline } KMnO_4} \underset{\text{Ethanoic acid}}{CH_3COOH} + \underset{\text{Water}}{H_2O}$$

Q.9 The mixture of oxygen and ethyne is burnt for welding. Can you tell why a mixture of ethyne and air is not used?

Ans. A mixture of ethyne and air is not used for welding, because burning of ethyne in air produces a sooty flame due to incomplete combustion which is not enough to melt metals for welding.
When ethyne is burnt is oxygen, large quantity of heat alongwith light is produced. The heat evolved can be used for gas welding which is usually carried to weld small broken pieces of articles made up of iron. Air mainly contains a mixture of nitrogen (4 parts) and oxygen (1 part). As we know, nitrogen gas does not support combustion. This means that in air, only oxygen will help in the combustion of ethyne. Therefore, it is always better to use oxygen for the combustion of ethyne.

Q.10 How would you distinguish experimentally between an alcohol and a carboxylic acid?

Ans. Take the samples of alcohol and carboxylic acid in different test tubes and add sodium hydrogen carbonate in both the test tubes.
The test tube from which the effervescence evolves is carboxylic acid. The effervescence is due to the evolution of carbon dioxide.

$$CH_3COOH + NaHCO_3 \longrightarrow CH_3COONa + H_2O + CO_2$$
$$C_2H_5OH + NaHCO_3 \longrightarrow \text{No evolution of } CO_2$$

Q.11 What are oxidising agents?

Ans. An oxidising agent is one which oxidizes other substances by providing oxygen or removing hydrogen. The Commonly used oxidising agent are : Ozone, bromine water, a mixture of potassium dichromate and sulphuric acid or a mixture of potassium permanganate and sulphuric acid.

Q.12 Would you be able to check if water is hard by using a detergent?

Ans. No, we cannot check the presence of hard water by using a detergent. Actually detergents produce foam in any type of water; whether hard or soft. Therefore, a distinction between the two cannot be made. However, soaps can be used for this purpose.

Q.13 People use a variety of methods to wash clothes. Usually after adding the soap, they 'beat' the clothes on a stone, or beat it with a paddle, scrub wit a brush or the mixture is agitated in a washing machine. Why is agitation necessary to get clean clothes?

Ans. The molecules of soap are sodium or potassium salts of long-chain carboxylic acids. The ionic-end of soap dissolves in water while the carbon chain dissolves in oil. The soap molecules, thus form structures called micelles. When cloth is agitated, the micelles containing oily or greasy dirt particles get removed from the surface of dirty cloth and into water and clothes gets cleaned.

Q.14 Ethane with the molecular formula C_2H_6 has

(A) 6 covalent bonds (B) 7 covalent bonds (C) 8 covalent bonds (D) 9 covalent bonds.

Ans. (B) [Hint : The structure of C_2H_6 is :

$$\begin{array}{ccccccc} & & H & & H & & \\ & & | & & | & & \\ H & - & C & - & C & - & H \\ & & | & & | & & \\ & & H & & H & & \end{array}$$

Q.15 Butanone is a four-carbon compound with the functional group

(A) carboxylic acid (B) aldehyde (C) ketone (D) alcohol

Ans. (C) [Hint : The structure of butanone is

$$\begin{array}{c} \quad\ \ O \\ \quad\ \ || \\ CH_3 - C - CH_2 - CH_3 \end{array}$$

Q.16 While cooking , if the bottom of the vessel is getting blackened on the outside it means that

(A) the food is not cooked completely (B) the fuel is not burning completely

(C) the fuel is wet (D) the fuel is burning completely

Ans. (B) The fuel is not burning completely.

Q.17 Explain the nature of the covalent bond using the bond formation in CH_3Cl.

Ans. Covalent bond is formed by sharing the electrons between two atoms:

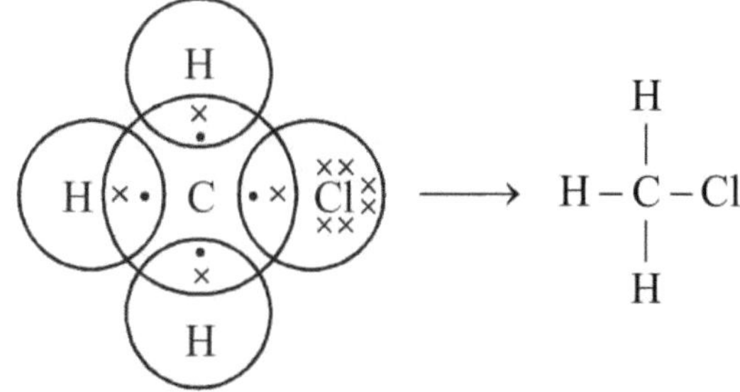

Q.18 Draw the electron dot structure for
(a) ethanoic acid (b) H_2S (c) propanone (d) F_2

Ans. The electron dot structures are given below:

(a) Ethanoic acid :

```
     H   ••                        H   O
     ×   O:                        |   ||
     •   ••     ••                 |   ||
H×•C••C••O•×H  ⟶  H – C – C – O – H
     •          ••                 |
     ×                             |
     H                             H
```

(b) Hydrogen sulphide :

```
     ••
H×•S•×H  ⟶  H – S – H
     ••
```

(c) Propanone :

```
     H  ×O×  H               H   O   H
     ×  ××   ×               |   ||  |
     •  ••   •               |   ||  |
H×•C••C••C•×H  ⟶  H – C – C – C – H
     •       •               |       |
     ×       ×               |       |
     H       H               H       H
```

(d) Fluorine :

```
 ••  ••
:F••F:  ⟶  F – F
 ••  ••
```

Q.19 What is an homologous series? Explain with an example.

Ans. A series of compounds in which the same functional group substitutes for hydrogen in a carbon chain is called homologous series. These differ by – CH_2 -unit.
Example: Homologous series of alcohols: CH_3OH, C_2H_5OH, C_3H_7OH. These differ by –CH_2-unit.

Q.20 How can ethanol and ethanoic acid be differentiated on the basis of their physical and chemical properties?

Ans. Differentiation of ethanol and ethanoic acid on the basis of their physical properties: Ethanol has a pleasant odour whereas Ethanoic acid smells like vinegar. Differentiation of ethanol and ethanoic acid on the basis of their chemical properties:
Take the samples of ethanol and ethanoic acid in different test tubes and add sodium hydrogen carbonate in both the test tubes. The test tube from which the effervescence evolves is ethanoic acid. The effervescence is due to the evolution of carbon dioxide.

$$CH_3COOH + NaHCO_3 \longrightarrow CH_3COONa + H_2O + CO_2$$
$$C_2H_5OH + NaHCO_3 \longrightarrow \text{No evolution of } CO_2$$

Q.21 Why does micelle formation take place when soap is added to water? Will a micelle be formed in other solvents such as ethanol also?

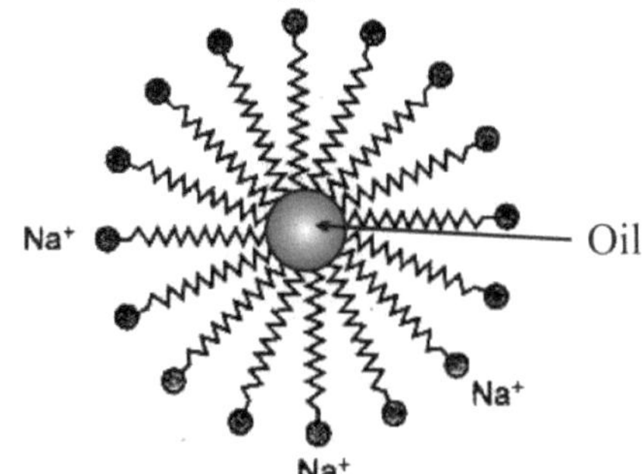

Ans. Soap are sodium or potassium salts of long-chain carboxylic acids. The acid end of soap dissolves in water while the carbon chain dissolves in oil. When soap is added to the water, the hydrophilic end (acid end) will align along the surface of water and the hydrophobic tail (carbon chain) remains out of water. The cluster of molecules in which hydrophobic tail are in the interior of cluster and the ionic ends are on the surface of cluster is called micelle (see fig.). The soap micelles thus helps in dissolving the dirt in water and we can wash our clothes clean. No, micelle will not be formed in other solvents such as ethanol because hydrocarbon chain of soap molecules are soluble in organic solvents like ethanol.

Q.22 Why are carbon and its compounds used as fuels for most applications?

Ans. Carbon and its compounds are used as a fuel because when they are burnt, they give large amount of energy in the form of heat.

Q.23 Explain the formation of scum when hard water is treated with soap.

Ans. Hard water contains soluble salts of sulphates and chlorides of calcium and magnesium. When soap is used to clean using hard water calcium and magnesium present in hard water produce an insoluble substance called scum that remains after washing the cloth with water.

$$\underset{\text{(Hard water)}}{Ca^{2+}} + \underset{\text{(Soap)}}{2RCOONa} \longrightarrow \underset{\substack{\text{Cal. salt (ppt.)} \\ \text{(Scum)}}}{(RCOO)_2Ca} + 2Na^+$$

$$\underset{\text{(Hard water)}}{Mg^{2+}} + \underset{\text{(Soap)}}{2RCOONa} \longrightarrow \underset{\substack{\text{Mag. salt (ppt.)} \\ \text{(Scum)}}}{(RCOO)_2Ca} + 2Na^+$$

Q.24 What change will you observe if you test soap with litmus paper (red and blue)?

Ans. When we test soap with red and blue litmus paper red will turn into blue but blue litmus will remain as blue.

Q.25 What is hydrogenation? What is its industrial application ?

Ans. Addition of hydrogen to an unsaturated hydrocarbon in presence of catalyst such as palladium or nickel to give saturated hydrocarbons is called hydrogenation. The process is used to make healthy vegetable oils in industry.

Q.26 Which of the following hydrocarbons undergo addition reactions: C_2H_6, C_3H_8, C_3H_6, C_2H_2 and CH_4.

Ans. Unsaturated hydrocarbons undergo addition reactions. The following are the unsaturated hydrocarbons amongst the given examples: C_3H_6 and C_2H_2.

Q.27 Give a test that can be used to differentiate chemically between butter and cooking oil.

Ans. Take butter and cooking oil in two separate test tubes. Add bromine water to each test tube. The one containing cooking oil will decolourise the light brown colour of bromine water, i.e., bromine water will become colourless. The colour of Bromine water will remain as such in other test tube.

Q.28 Explain the mechanism of the cleaning action of soaps.

Ans. Cleaning action of soap has been explained with the help of fig. Soaps are molecules in which the two ends have differing properties, one is hydrophilic, that is it dissolves in water, while the other end is hydrophobic, that is it dissolves in hydrocarbons. When soap is at the surface of water the hydrophobic 'tail' of soap will not be soluble in water and the soap will align along the surface of water with the ionic ed in water and the hydrocarbon 'tail' protruding out of water. Inside water, these molecules have a unique orientation that keeps the hydrocarbon portion out of the water. This is achieved by forming clusters of molecules in which the hydrophobic tails are in the interior of the cluster and the ionic ends are on the surface of the cluster. This formation is called a micelle. Soap in the form of a micelle is able to clean, since the oily dirt will be collected in the centre of the micelle. The micelles are large enough to scatter light. Hence a soap solution appears cloudy.

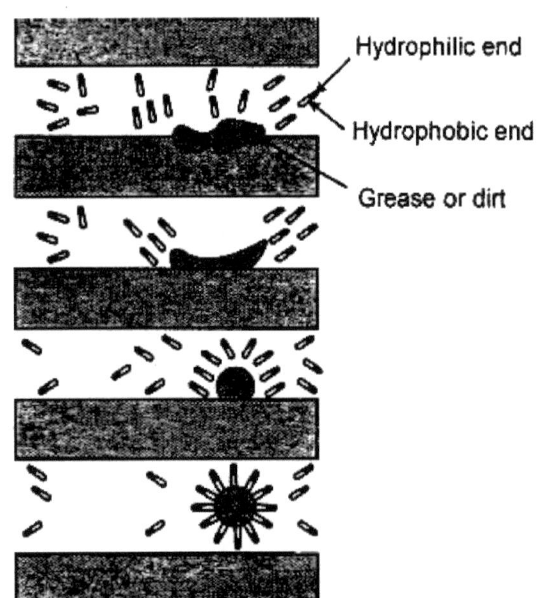

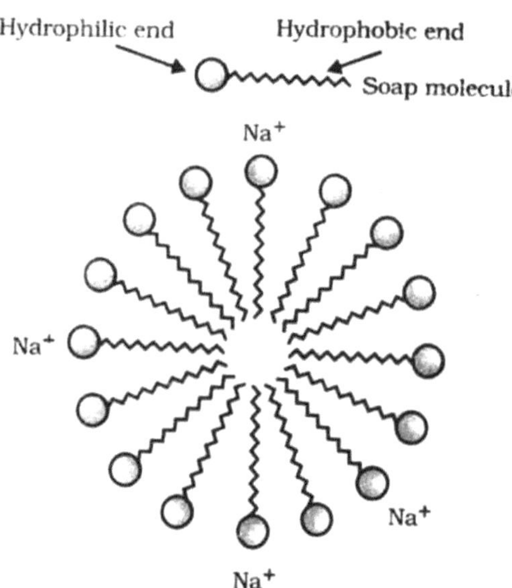

CONCEPT APPLICATION LEVEL - II [Previous Year Questions]

SECTION-A

- **Multiple Choice Questions (one correct answer) :**

Q.1 A few drops of ethanoic acid were added to solid sodium carbonate. The observation made was that.
(A) a hissing sound was produced (B) brown fumes were evolved
(C) brisk effervescence occurred. (D) a pungent smelling was evolved

Q.2 The chemical formula of glyceryl palmitate is :
(A) $(C_{17}H_{33}\ COO)_3C_3H_5$ (B) $(C_{17}H_{35}COO)_3C_3H_5$
(C) $(C_{15}H_{32}\ COO)_3C_3H_5$ (D) none of these

Q.3 The by product obtained during the preparation of soap is :
(A) glycol (B) glycerol (C) glycerine (D) any of (B) or (C)

Q.4 The function of sodium hydroxide solution in the making of soap is to :
(A) neutralize the vegetable oils (B) hydrolyse the vegetable oils.
(C) dehydrate the vegetable oils (D) oxidise the vegetable oils.

Q.5 To the washed soap are added dyes, perfumes or any other desired materials which are commonly called.
(A) preservatives (B) drying agents. (C) fillers (D) none of these

Q.6 In the following experimental set up, the gas evolved burns with a pop sound. Identify X.

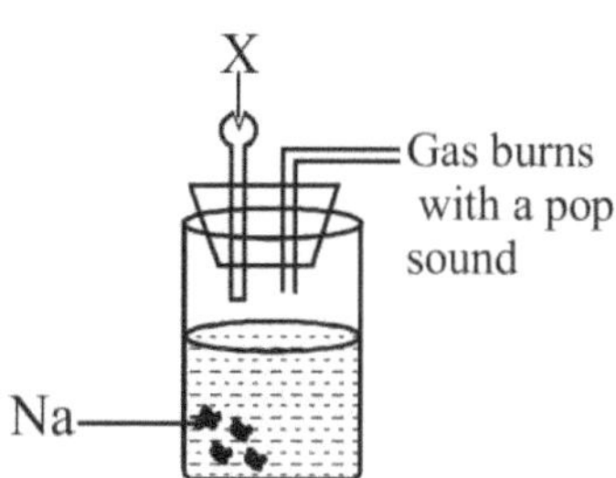

(A) $NaHCO_3$ (B) CH_3COOH (C) NH_4OH (D) $CH_3COOC_2H_5$

Q.7 Acetic acid was added to a solid X kept in a test tube. A colourless, odour less gas Y was evolved. The gas was passed through lime water, which turned lime water milky. It was concluded that
(A) solid X is sodium hydroxide and the gas Y is CO_2.
(B) solid X is sodium bicarbonate and the gas Y is CO_2.
(C) solid X is sodium acetate and the gas Y is CO_2.
(D) solid X is sodium bicarbonate and the gas Y is SO_2.

Q.8 The molecular formulae of some organic compounds are given below. Which of the se compounds contains an aldehyde group?
(A) C_3H_8O (B) $C_3H_6O_2$ (C) C_3H_6O (D) C_3H_7Cl

Q.9 Ethanoic acid was added to sodium bicarbonate solution and the gas evolved was tested with a burning splinter. The following four observation were reported.
(a) The gas burns with the pop sound and the flame gets extinguished.
(b) The gas does not burn but the splinter burns with a pop sound.
(c) the flame extinguishes and the gas does not burn.
(d) The gas burns with a blue flame and the splinter burns brightly.
The correct observation is reported in :
(A) (a) (B) (b) (C) (c) (D) (d)

Q.10 When groundnut oil is heated with caustic soda solution, the products which are formed are
(A) a soap and glycerol (B) a detergent and glycerol
(C) only a soap (D) only a detergent.

Q.11 Glacial acetic acid be :
(A) 5-8% acetic acid (B) 50% acetic acid
(C) 100% acetic acid (D) acetic acid of any concentration.

SECTION-B

- **Very Short Answer type Questions** **[1 Mark]**

Q.12 What happens when a small piece of sodium is dropped into ethanol?
Ans. Hydrogen gas is evolved with the formation of sodium ethoxide.

$$\underset{\text{Sodium metal}}{Na} + \underset{\text{Ethanol}}{C_2H_5OH} \rightarrow \underset{\text{Sodium ethoxide}}{C_2H_5ONa} + \underset{\text{Hydrogen gas}}{H_2 \uparrow}$$

Q.13 What is the difference between two consecutive members in a homologous series in alkanes in terms of
(i) molecular mass.
(ii) numbers of atoms of elements
Ans. (i) 14 u
(ii) CH_2(1 atom of carbon and 2 atoms of hydrogen)

Q.14 The molecular formula of A is $C_{10}H_{18}$ and B is $C_{18}H_{36}$. Name the homologous series in which they belong?
Ans. A belongs to homologous series of Alkynes having general formula C_nH_{2n-2}.
B belongs to homologous series of alkenes having general formula C_nH_{2n}

Q.15 Why are soaps ineffective in hard water?
Ans. Soaps react with Calcium (Ca^{2+}) and magnesium (Mg^{2+}) ions present in hard water to form insoluble precipitates called soap scum

$$\underset{\text{Soap molcule}}{2C_{17}H_{35}COO^-Na^+} + \underset{\text{(ions present in hard water)}}{Cu^{2+} / Mg^{2+}} \rightarrow \underset{\text{Soap scum (Water insoluble)}}{(C_{17}H_{35}COO^-)Ca^{2+}}$$

Q.16 Write the name of the following?

(i) CH_3CH_2COOH

(ii) $CH_3CH_2CH_2Br$

Ans. (i) Propanoic acid

(ii) Bromopropane

Q.17 What will you observe on adding a 5% alkaline potassium permanganate solution drop by drop to some warm ethanol taken in a test tube? write the same of the compound formed during the above chemical reaction?

Ans. On adding $KMnO_4$, the pink colour of $KMnO_4$ disappears initial because it oxidises ethanol in ethanoic acid. Name of the substance formed : **Ethanoic acid**.

Q.18 Saturated hydrocarbons burn with a blue flame while unsaturated hydrocarbons burn with a sooty flame? Why?

Ans. Unsaturated hydrocarbons burn with a sooty flame because of incomplete combustion due to which unburned carbon particles are left making the flame sooty.

Q.19 Why do carbon compounds not conduct electricity?

Ans. Since carbon compounds do not give rise to any ions or charged particles in molten state or in aqueous solutions.

Q.20 How ethanoic acid get its name as glacial acetic acid?

Ans. The melting point of ethanoic acid is 290 K and hence it often freezes during winter and form ice like flakes.

(2 Marks question)

Q.21 What are heteroatoms ? What is their importance?

Ans. The elements such as halogens, nitrogen, oxygen and sulphur those replace hydrogen atoms in a hydrocarbon chain are called heteroatoms. These heteroatoms confer specific properties to the compound, regardless of the length and nature of the carbon chain and hence, they are also called as functional groups.

Q.22 State one point of difference between soap and synthetic detergent.

Ans.

	Soap		**Synthetic**
1.	Soap is a sodium or potassium salt of long –chain carboxylic acid.	1.	Detergent is a ammonium or sulphonate salt of long-chain carboxylic acid.
2.	Soap form scum with hard water and thus cannot be used for washing with hard water.	2.	Detergent do not form insoluble precipitates(scum) with the calcium and magnesium ions in hard water and thus they can be used with hard water.
3.	Soaps are more biodegradable	3.	Detergents are less biodegradable.

Q.23 What is meant by hydration of ethene? Explain.

Ans. Most of the ethanol used for commercial purpose is produced by hydration of ethene. This process involves reaction of ethene with water in the presence of concentrated sulphuric acid.

$$\underset{\text{Ethene}}{H_2C=CH_2}+H_2O \xrightarrow{\text{conc.}H_2SO_4} \underset{\text{Ethanol}}{H_3C-CH_2-OH}$$

Q.24 Complete the following equations:

(i) $CH_3COOH + KHCO_3 \rightarrow$

(i) $CH_4 + Cl_2 \rightarrow$

Ans. (i) $CH_3COOH + KHCO_3 \rightarrow \quad CH_3COOK + H_2O + CO_2$

(i) $CH_4 + Cl_2 \xrightarrow{\text{Sunlight}} CH_3Cl + HCl$

Q.25 What happens when - (Given equations also) -

(i) Methane reacts with excess of chlorine in the presence of diffused sunlight.

(ii) Ethanol undergoes combustion.

(iii) Ethyl alcohol reacts with acidified potassium dichromate.

Ans. (i) $CH_4 + 4Cl_2 \xrightarrow{\text{Diffused Sunlight}} CCl_4 + 4HCl$

(ii) $CH_3CH_2OH + 3O_2 \rightarrow 3CO_2 + 3H_2O + \text{Heat and light}$

(iii) $CH_3CH_2OH + [O] \xrightarrow{\text{Acidified } K_2Cr_2O_7} CH_3-\underset{\underset{O}{\|}}{C}-OH + H_2O$

Q.26 Give two reasons to explain why carbon forms large number of compounds.

Ans. (i) Carbon has the unique ability to form bonds with other atoms of carbon giving rise to large molecules. This property is called catenation.

(ii) Carbon has a valency of four (tetra valency) and it has a small size. This enables carbon to form very strong bonds with other elements.

Q.27 Why does miclle formation take place when soap is added to water? will a micelle be formed in other solvents such as ethanol also?

Ans. A soap has two parts:

(a) A polar, water soluble, hydrophilic acid.

(b) A nonpolar, water - insoluble hydrophobic acid.

So when soap is added to water polar ends dissolve in water whereas nonpolar do not. Hence, spherical structures are formed called as Micelle. But in ethanol, soap is soluble, hence micelle are not formed.

Q.28 Two compounds X and Y have the same molecular formula C_3H_6O. Write their structures and name of the functional groups present in them. Also give their IUPAC names.

Ans.

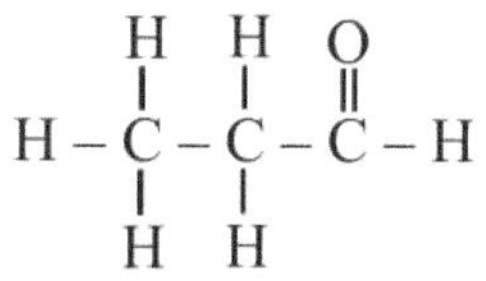

$$H-\overset{H}{\underset{H}{C}}-\overset{H}{\underset{H}{C}}-\overset{O}{\overset{\|}{C}}-H$$

Propanal(X)

$$H-\overset{H}{\underset{H}{C}}-\overset{O}{\overset{\|}{C}}-\overset{H}{\underset{H}{C}}-H$$

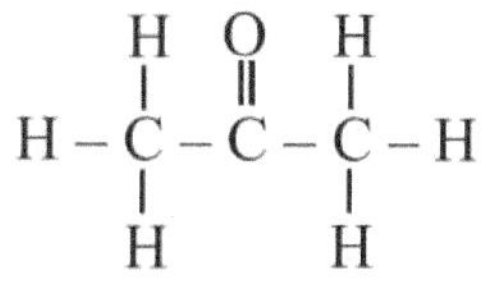

Propanone(Y)

Propanal(X) contains aldehyde group, i.e. $-\overset{O}{\overset{\|}{C}}-H$ as the functional group while propanone (Y) contains keto group ($>C=O$) as functional group.

Q.29 Write equation for the chemical reaction which shows the acidic nature of ethanol.

Ans. Na is a stronger base. It reacts with ethanol to form H_2 gas. Therefore, ethanol must be an acid.

$$\underset{\text{Ethanol}}{2CH_3CH_2OH} + 2Na \rightarrow \underset{\text{Sod.ethoxide}}{2CH_3CH_2ON} + H_2$$

Q.30 **Fill in the blanks :**

(a) Ethene and ethyne are examples of_____ hydrocarbons.

(b) C_nH_{2n} is the general formula for______

(c) Hydrocarbons having the general formula C_nH_{2n-2} are called______

(d) A double bond between two carbon atoms is formed when each carbon shares_____electrons.

(e) Compounds having the same molecular formula but different arrangement of atoms within their molecules are called_________

Ans. (a) Unsaturated (b) alkenes of cycloalkanes (c) alkynes (d) two (e) isomers

- **Short Answer type Questions** **[3 Mark]**

Q.31 Write two isomers having the molecular formula, CH_4N_2O ? Which of the two is an ionic and which is the covalent compound? How will you prepare them in the laboratory?

Ans. The two isomeric compounds are

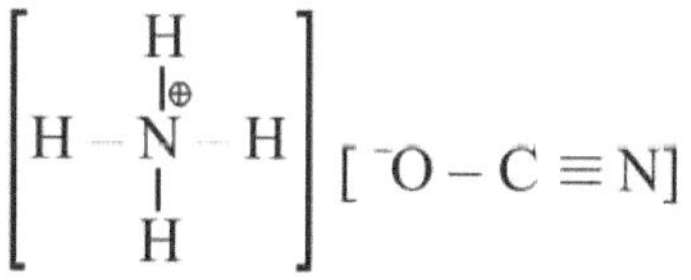

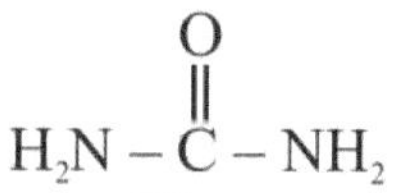

$$\left[H-\overset{H}{\underset{H}{\overset{|\oplus}{N}}}-H\right][^-O-C\equiv N] \qquad \underset{\text{Urea}}{H_2N-\overset{O}{\overset{\|}{C}}-NH_2}$$

Ammonium cyanate is an ionic compound while urea is a covalent compound. Ammonium cyanate is obtained when an aqueous solution of ammonium chloride and potassium cyanate is heated. It is an unstable compound. Therefore, on further heating, it undergoes a rearrangement reaction to form urea.

$$\underset{\text{Amm.Chloride}}{NH_4Cl} + \underset{\text{Pot.cyanate}}{KNCO} \xrightarrow{\text{heat}} \underset{\text{Amm.cyanate}}{NH_4CNO} + \underset{\text{Pot.chloride}}{KCl}$$

$$\underset{\text{Amm.Chloride}}{NH_4CNO} \xrightarrow{\text{heat}} \underset{\text{Urea}}{HN_2-CO-NH_2}$$

Q.32 What is the difference between combustion and oxidation? Under what conditions, and oxidation reaction can be called as combustion? Illustrate your answer with one example in each case.

Ans. Addition of oxygen or removal of hydrogen from any substance is called oxidation. For example, when ethanol is burnt in air, it produces CO_2 and H_2O.

$$\underset{\text{Ethanol}}{CH_3CH_2OH} + 3O_2 \longrightarrow \underset{\text{Carbon dioxide}}{2CO_2} + 3H_2O$$

However, when ethanol is heated with alk. $KMnO_4$ or acidified $K_2Cr_2O_7$, it gives ethanoic acid.

$$\underset{\text{Ethanol}}{CH_3CH_2OH} + 2[O] \xrightarrow[\text{or } K_2Cr_2O_7/H_2SO_4,\text{Heat}]{KMnO_4,KOH,\text{Heat}} \underset{\text{Ethanoic acid}}{CH_3COOH} + H_2O$$

Both these reactions are oxidation reactions because in both the cases oxygen has been added or hydrogen has been removed. But complete oxidation of an organic compound to form CO_2 and H_2O is called combustion. Therefore, oxidation of ethanol to form CO_2 and H_2O can also be called as combustion reaction. Thus, complete oxidation of an organic compound to form CO_2 and H_2O is also called combustion while partial oxidation of a compound to give a compound other than CO_2 and H_2O is only called oxidation.

Q.33 Two compound X and Y have the same molecular formula C_6H_{12}. Compound X is saturated while compound Y is unsaturated. Draw their structures. What type of reactions, compounds X and Y are expected to undergo?

Ans. The molecular formula, C_6H_{12} corresponds to the general formula C_nH_{2n} characteristic of cycloalkanes and alkenes. Since compound X is saturated, It must be cyclohexane and since compound Y is unsaturated it must be 1-hexene or any other isomeric hexene. Their structure are :

```
         H  H
          \/
          C
  H\    /   \    /H
 H—C          C—H
    |          |
 H—C          C—H
  H/    \   /    \H
          C
          /\
         H  H
```

Cyclohexane(X)

```
     H   H   H   H   H   H
     |   |   |   |   |   |
 H - C - C - C - C - C = C - H
     |   |   |   |   |
     H   H   H   H   H
```

1-Hexene(Y)

Since compound X is saturated having only C – C single bonds, it is expected to undergo substitution reactions.

Since compound Y is unsaturated having one C = C single bonds, it is expected to undergo substitution reactions.

Q.34 Two carbon compounds A and B have the molecular formula C_3H_8 and C_3H_6 respectively. Which one of the two is most likely to show addition reaction? Justify your answer .Explain with the help of a chemical equation, how an addition is useful in vegetable ghee industry.

Ans. C_3H_8 corresponds to the general formula C_nH_{2n+2} (n = 3), therefore, it is an alkane which is a saturated compound. The molecular formula, C_3H_6 corresponds to the general formual C_nH_{2n} (n = 3), therefore, it is an alkene which is an unsaturated compound. Since alkenes contain a double bond, therefore, C_3H_6 is more reactive than C_3H_8. They add H_2 in presence of a catalyst (nickel) to form saturated hydrocarbons. For example,

$$H-\underset{\substack{|\\H}}{\overset{\substack{H\\|}}{C}}-\overset{\substack{H\\|}}{C}=\overset{\substack{H\\|}}{C}-H + H_2 \xrightarrow[473K]{Nickel} H-\underset{\substack{|\\H}}{\overset{\substack{H\\|}}{C}}-\underset{\substack{|\\H}}{\overset{\substack{H\\|}}{C}}-\underset{\substack{|\\H}}{\overset{\substack{H\\|}}{C}}-H$$

Propene(C_3H_6) Propene(C_3H_8)

This addition reaction is useful in industry for converting vegetable oil to vanaspati ghee.

Vegetable oils contain a number of unsaturated carbon chains having double bonds between carbon atoms. When H_2 gas is bubbled through vegetable oils in presence of nickel as catalyst at 473 K, some of these double bonds add H_2 to form saturated carbon chains. As a result of this partial hydrogenations, vegetable oils are converted into solid vanaspati ghee.

Q.35 An organic compound A is widely used as preservative in pickles and has a molecular formula C_2H_4O. This compound reacts with ethanol to form a sweet smelling compound B.

(i) Identify the compound A

(ii) Write the chemical equation for its reaction with ethanol to form compound B.

(iii) How can we get compound A back from B?

(iv) Name the process and write corresponding chemical equation.

Ans. (i) The compound A is ethanoic acid commonly known as acetic acid having formula as : CH_3COOH.

(ii) $$\underset{\text{Ethanoic acid}}{CH_3COOH} + \underset{\text{Ethanol}}{C_2H_5OH} \xrightarrow[\text{Sulphuric acid}]{\text{Esterfication}} \underset{\substack{\text{Ethyl ethanoate}\\\text{(Compound B)}}}{CH_3COOC_2H_5} + H_2O$$

(iii) The above process is known as hydrolysis of an ester.

$$\underset{\text{Compound B}}{CH_3COOC_2H_5} \xrightarrow{\text{NaOH}} \underset{\text{Compound A}}{CH_3COOH} + C_2H_5OH$$

(iv) CO_2 is produced when the compound A reacts with washing soda (Na_2CO_3)

$$\underset{\text{Ethanoic acid}}{2CH_3COOH} + \underset{\text{Washing soda}}{Na_2CO_3} \longrightarrow \underset{\text{Sodium ethanoate}}{2CH_3COONa} + H_2O + CO_2$$

Q.36 An organic compound A is an essential constituent of wine and beer. Oxidation of A yield on organic acid B which is present in vinegar. Name the compounds A and B and write their structural formula. What happens when A and B react in the presence of an acid catalyst? Write the chemical equation for the reaction.

Ans. Ethyl alcohol is an essential constituent of wine and beer. Therefore A is ethyl alcohol. Oxidation of ethyl alcohol gives acetic acid. Vinegar contains acetic. Therefore, B is acetic acid.

$$\begin{array}{ccccc} & H & & H & \\ & | & & | & \\ H - & C & - & C & - OH \\ & | & & | & \\ & H & & H & \end{array} \qquad \begin{array}{ccccc} & H & & & \\ & | & & & \\ H - & C & - & C & - OH \\ & | & & \| & \\ & H & & O & \end{array}$$

Ethyl alcohol (A) Acetic acid (B)

When A and B react in the presence of an acid catalyst, the ester, ethyl acetate is formed.

$$\underset{\text{Ethyl alcohol}}{CH_3CH_2OH} + \underset{\text{Acetic acid}}{CH_3COOH} \xrightarrow{\text{conc.} H_2SO_4} \underset{\text{ethyl acetate}}{CH_3COOC_2H_5} + H_2O$$

Q.37 (a) Distinguish between esterification and saponification reactions of organic compounds.
(b) With a labelled diagram describe on activity to show the formation of an ester.

OR

Describe an activity to show the formation of an ester in the school laboratory?

Ans. (a) A chemical reaction in which an alcohol reacts with alkanoic acid to form a sweet smelling compound (ester) is called esterification.

$$\underset{\text{Ethanoic acid}}{CH_3COOH} + \underset{\text{Ethanol}}{C_2H_5OH} \xrightarrow[\text{Warming}]{\text{conc.} H_2SO_4} \underset{\substack{\text{Ethyl ethanoate} \\ \text{(ester)}}}{CH_3COOC_2H_5} + H_2O$$

A chemical reaction in which an ester gets hydrolysed in the presence of sodium hydroxide to form the constituent alcohol and sodium salt of the alkanoic acid is called saponification.

$$\underset{\text{Ethyl ethanoate}}{CH_3COOC_2H_5} + \underset{\text{Sodium hydroxide}}{NaOH} \rightarrow \underset{\text{Sodium acetate}}{CH_3COONa} + \underset{\text{Ethanol}}{C_2H_5OH}$$

(b) **Activity**

* Pour 1 ml of ethanol (absolute alcohol in a test tube)
* Pour 1 ml of glacial acetic acid in the alcohol and then a few drops of conc. sulphuric acid.
* Warm the contents of the test tube in a hot water bath for 10 min.
* Pour the contents of the test tube in another beaker containing 20 ml of water.
* Smell the contents of the beaker. You will find a sweet fruity smell. This smell is due to the formation of the ester, ethyl ethanoate.

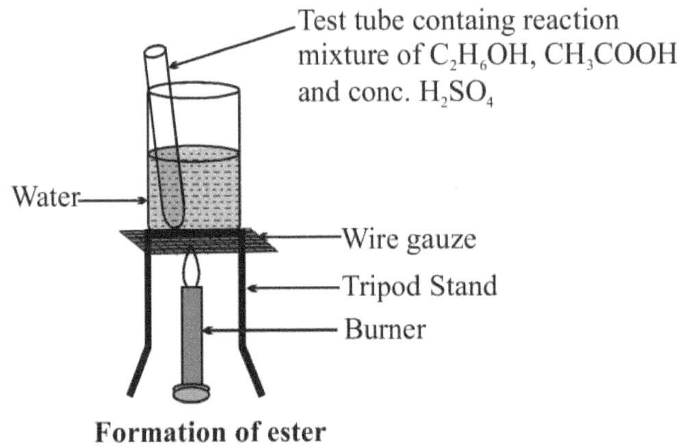

Formation of ester

Q.38 Name the oxidising agent used for the conversion of ethanol to ethanoic acid. Distinguish between and ethanoic acid on the basis of

(i) Litmus test (ii) reaction with sodium carbonate.

Ans. The oxidising agent used for the conversion of ethanol to ethanoic acid - potassium permanganate($KMnO_4$)

(i) **Litmus test :** Ethanol shows no effect on blue or red litmus paper, so it acts as a neutral towards the litmus paper, while ethanoic acid changes blue litmus into red so it is acidic.

(ii) **Reaction of sodium carbonate** : Ethanol does not react with sodium carbonate, while, ethanoic acid liberates carbon dioxide on reacting with sodium carbonate.

$$\underset{\text{(ethanol)}}{C_2H_5OH} + \underset{\text{(Sodium carbonate)}}{Na_2CO_3} \rightarrow \text{No reaction}$$

$$\underset{\text{(Ethanoic acid)}}{2CH_3COOH} + \underset{\text{(Sodium carbonate)}}{Na_2CO_3} \rightarrow 2CH_3COONa + H_2O + CO_2$$

Q.39 Explain the given reactions with examples :

(a) (i) oxidation reaction (ii) Substitution reaction (iii) Addition reaction

(b) What is glacial acetic acid ? Why is it named so? State its two uses.

Ans. (a) (i) Ehtanol is oxidised to ethanoic acid in the presence of alkaline $KMnO_4$ on beating.

$$CH_3CH_2OH \xrightarrow[\text{Heat}]{\text{Alk.KMnO}_4} CH_3COOH$$

(ii) In the presence of sunlight, chlorine replaces all the atoms of hydrogen in a hydrocarbon.

$$CH_4 + Cl_2 \xrightarrow[\text{HCl}]{\text{hv}} CH_3Cl \xrightarrow[\text{HCl}]{\text{hv}} CH_2Cl_2 \xrightarrow[\text{HCl}]{\text{hv}} CHCl_3 \xrightarrow[\text{HCl}]{\text{hv}} CCl_4$$

(iii) Ethene add hydrogen in presence of heat nickel or palladium to form ethane.

$$C_2H_4 + H_2 \xrightarrow{\text{Ni}-300°\text{C}} C_2H_6$$

(b) Ethanoic acid freezes below 16.5°C to form an icy mass, which is know as glacial acetic acid. It looks icy so, named glacial acetic acid. Its two uses are

(i) In the formation of vinegar.

(ii) As a solvent for a large number of organic compounds

Q.40 An organic compound A having molecular formula $C_2H_4O_2$ reacts with sodium metal and evolves a gas B which readily catches fire. A also reacts with ethanol in the presence of concentrated sulphuric acid in form sweet smelling substance C used in making perfumes.

(i) Identify the compounds A, B and C.

(ii) Write balanced chemical equations to represent the conversion of :

(a) Compound A into compound B.

(b) Compound A into compound C.

Ans. (i) Compound A is CH_3COOH (Ethanoic acid)

Compound B is H_2(Hydrogen gas)

Compound C is $CH_3-COOC_2H_5$ (Ethyl ethanoate)

(ii) (a) $$\underset{\text{compound A}}{2CH_3COOH} + 2Na \xrightarrow{\text{conc.H}_2\text{SO}_4} 2CH_3COONa + \underset{\text{compound B}}{H_2}$$

(b) $$\underset{\text{compound A}}{CH_3COOH} + C_2H_5OH \xrightarrow{\text{conc.H}_2\text{SO}_4} \underset{\text{compound C}}{CH_3COOC_2H_5} + H_2O$$

- **Long Answer type Questions** **[5 Mark]**

Q.41 An organic compound 'X' on heating with conc. H_2SO_4 forms a compound 'Y' which on addition of one molecule of hydrogen in the presence of nickel forms a compound 'Z'. One molecule of compound 'Z' on combustion forms two molecules of CO_2 and three molecules of H_2O. Identify giving reasons the compounds 'X', 'Y' and 'Z'. Write the chemical equations for all the chemical reactions involved.

Ans. Since compound Z gives 3 molecules of CO_2 and 3 molecules of H_2O, it shows that it has the molecular formula C_2H_6 (ethane). Z is obtained by the addition of one molecule of hydrogen to compound Y so the molecular formula of Y should be C_2H_4 (ethene). Compound Y is obtained by heating compound X with concentrated H_2SO_4 which shows it to be an alcohol. So compound X could e C_2H_5OH(ethanol).

$$C_2H_5OH\ (X) \xrightarrow{\text{Hot conc.} H_2SO_4} C_2H_4(Y) + H_2O$$

$$C_2H_4(Y) + H_2 \xrightarrow{Ni} C_2H_6(Z)$$

$$2C_2H_6(Z) + 7O_2 \rightarrow 4CO_2 + 6H_2O + \text{Heat and light}$$

Q.42 Explain the cleansing action of soap.

Ans. A molecule of soap is made up of two parts.

(i) An ionic part which is hydrophilic, i.e. water soluble.

(ii) A hydrocarbon chain which is hydrophobic i.e. water repelling and oil soluble.

Soap molecule

When soap is at the surface of water, the hydrophobic tail protrudes out of water while the ionic end remains inside water. Inside water, the molecules form clusters with the hydrophobic tails in the interior of the cluster and the ionic ends on the surface of the cluster. This formation is called a micelle. Soap, in the form of micelle collects the oily dirt in the centre of the micelle. The micelles stay in solution is a colloid and do not precipitate due to ion-ion repulsion. Thus, the dirt suspended in water is washed away during rinsing.

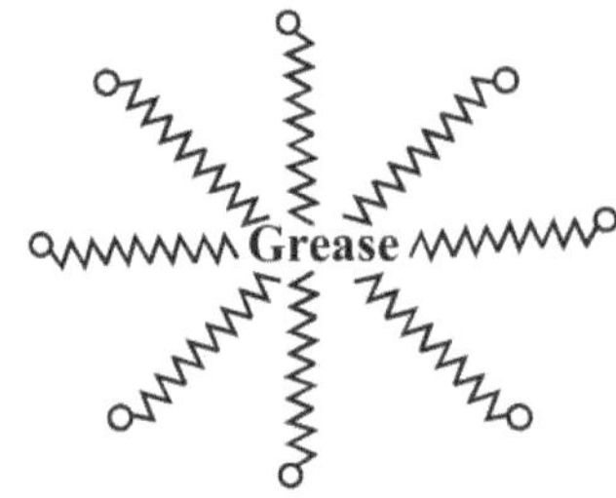

A micelle entrapping grease particle

Q.43 What is ethanol? State its two properties. What happens when it is heated with excess of conc. H_2SO_4 at 443K? What role does conc. H_2SO_4 play in this reaction? Write chemical equation of the reaction involved and the structural formula of the main product formed.

OR

An organic compound A is an essential constituent of wine and beer oxidation of A yields an organic acid B. Which is present in vinegar. Name the compounds A and B and write their structural formulae. What happens when A and B react in the presence of an acid catalyst? Write the chemical equation for the reaction.

Ans. Ethanol is an alcohol. its chemical formula is CH_3CH_2OH

Properties of ehtanol are :

(i) It is a colourless, volatile liquid having pleasant smell and burning taste.

(ii) it is miscible with water in all proportions

Dehydration : When ethanol is heated at 443 K (170°C) with excess of conc. sulphuric acid a water molecule is given out and ethene is formed.

$$\underset{\text{Ethanol}}{CH_3CH_2OH} \xrightarrow[443K]{\text{conc.}H_2SO_4} \underset{\text{Ethene}}{CH_2 = CH_2} + H_2O$$

Role of conc. H_2SO_4 : In this reaction, conc. H_2SO_4 acts as a dehydrating agent (a substance which is used to remove water molecule).

Structural formation of main product i.e. ethene.

$$\begin{array}{ccccc} H & & & & H \\ & \diagdown & & \diagup & \\ & & C = C & & \\ & \diagup & & \diagdown & \\ H & & & & H \end{array}$$

Ethene

OR

Organic compound A is ethanol. It is an essential constituent of wine and beer

Vinegar contains acetic acid. It is an organic acid oxidation of A yields an organic acid B which is present in vinegar. So, organic acid B is acetic acid

Structural formulae of compounds A and B are

$$\begin{array}{ccccccc} & H & & H & & \\ & | & & | & & \\ H - & C & - & C & - & OH \\ & | & & | & & \\ & H & & H & & \end{array} \qquad \begin{array}{ccccccc} & H & & O & & \\ & | & & \| & & \\ H - & C & - & C & - & O-H \\ & | & & & & \\ & H & & & & \end{array}$$

Ethanol (C_2H_5OH)
Compound A

Ethanoic acid (CH_3COOH)
Compound B

When A and B react in the presence of an acid catalyst, a pleasant smell of ester (ethyl ethanoate) is obtained.

$$\underset{A}{CH_3CH_2OH} + \underset{B}{CH_3COOH} \xrightarrow[\text{warm}]{\text{conc.}H_2SO_4} \underset{\text{Ethyl ethanoate (ester)}}{CH_3COOH_2CH_3} + H_2O$$

Q.44 (a) Write the name for the following compounds:

(i) $CH_3-\underset{\underset{CH_3}{|}}{CH}-CH_2-CH_3$ (ii) $CH_3-CH=CH-CH_2-CH_3$

(iii) $CH_3-\underset{\underset{O}{||}}{C}-CH_2-CH_3$ (iv) $CH_3-CH_2-\underset{\underset{Cl}{|}}{CH}-CH_3$

(b) (i) Take about 3 mL of ethanol in a test tube and warm it greatly in a water bath.

(ii) Add a 5% solution of alkaline potassium permanganate drop by drop to the solution.

(iii) What happens to the colour of $KMnO_4$ added initially and then in excess? Give reason. Name the product of this reaction.

Ans. (a) (i) 2 methyl butane (ii) Pent-2-ene

(iii) Butanone (iv) 2 Chlorobutane

(b) Initially colour of $KMnO_4$ is dark pink (magenta) which disappears on warming. When excess of $KMnO_4$ is added. the colour persists.

Reasons :

(i) $KMnO_4$ is dark pink in aqueous medium.

(ii) The colour disappears because it liberates nascent oxygen which is taken by ethanol and it gets oxidised to ethanoic acid.

(iii) When $KMnO_4$ is added in excess, more ethanol is not present in the mixture which can take up nascent oxygen from $KMnO_4$ and therefore, the colour persists.

The product of this reaction is : Ethanoic acid.

Q.45 An organic compound A is widely used as preservative in pickles and has a molecular formula C_2H_4O. This compound reacts with methanol to form a sweet smelling compound B.

(i) Identify the compound A

(ii) Write the chemical equation for its reaction with ethanol to form compound B.

(iii) How can we get compound A back from B?

(iv) Name the process and write corresponding chemical equation.

(v) Which gas is produced when compound A reacts with washing soda? Write the chemical equation.

Sol. (i) The compound A is ethanoic acid commonly known as acetic acid having formula as: CH_3COOH.

(ii) $$\underset{\text{Ethanoic Acid}}{CH_3COOH} + \underset{\text{Ethanol}}{C_2H_5OH} \xrightarrow{\text{Esterfication sulphuric acid}} \underset{\text{Ethyl ethanoate comound B}}{CH_3COOC_2H_5} + H_2O$$

(iii) We can get back compound A by treating compound B with NaOH.

(iv) The above process is known as hydrolysis of an ester.

$$\underset{\text{Compound B}}{CH_3COOC_2H_5} \xrightarrow{\text{NaOH}} \underset{\text{Compound A}}{CH_3COOH} + C_2H_5OH$$

(v) CO_2 is produced when the compound A reacts with washing soda (Na_2CO_3).

$$\underset{\text{Ethanoic Acid}}{2CH_3COOH} + \underset{\text{Washing Soda}}{Na_2CO_3} \rightarrow \underset{\text{Sodium ethanoate}}{2CH_3COONa} + H_2O + CO_2$$

CONCEPT APPLICATION LEVEL - III

Q.1 Out of the following the one that undergoes reaction with 50% NaOH solution to give corresponding alcohol and acid is : **[NSEJS-I-2008-9]**

(A) phenol (B) benzaldehyde (C) butanol (D) benzoic acid

Q.2 A carboxylic acid will evolve CO_2 when reacted with **[NSEJS-I-2008-9]**

(A) $NaHCO_3$ (B) HCl (C) $NaHSO_3$ (D) Na_2CO_3

Q.3 On mixing certain alkane with chlorine and irradiating with ultraviolet light, it forms only one monochloro alkane. This alkane could be : **[NSEJS-I-2009]**

(A) propane (B) pentane (C) isopentane (D) neopentane

Q.4 The isomerism which exists between CH_3CHCl_2 and CH_2ClCH_2Cl is **[NSEJS-I-2013-14]**

(A) chain isomerism (B) functional group isomerism

(C) positional isomerism (D) metamerism

Q.5 From the following pool of molecules **[NSEJS-I-2015-16]**

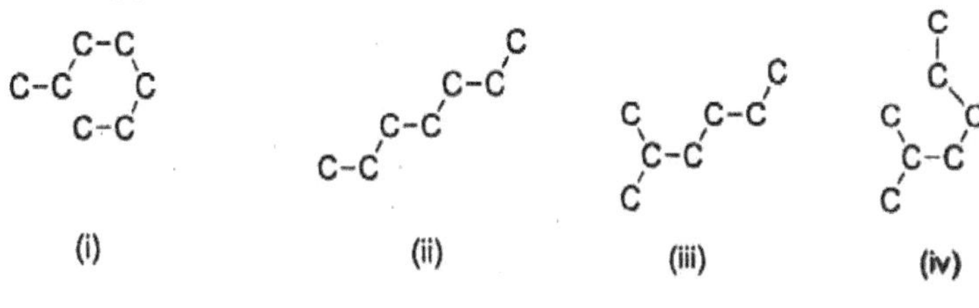

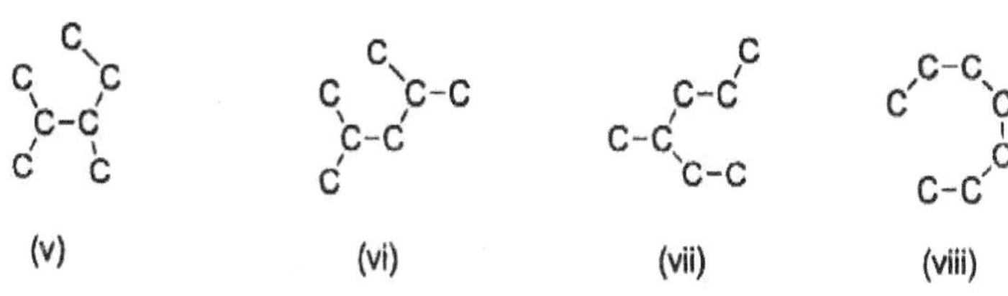

How many isomers are represented above

(A) 2 (B) 3 (C) 4 (D) 5

Q.6 Which compound dissolves in water to form an aqueous solution that can conduct an electric current? **[INJSO-I-2009]**

(A) CCl_4 (B) C_2H_5OH (C) CH_3COOH (D) CH_4

Q.7 Which compound has the empirical formula with the greatest mass ? **[INJSO_II-2009]**

(A) C_2H_6 (B) C_4H_{10} (C) C_5H_{10} (D) C_6H_6

Q.8 A white salt is readily soluble in water and gives colorless solution with pH of about 9. The salt would be **[INJSO_II-2012]**

(A) NH_4NO_3 (B) CH_3COONa (C) CH_3COONH_4 (D) $CaCO_2$

Q.9 Hydrogenation is a reaction in which hydrogen is added to a compound. One of the application of hydrogenation reaction is to convert unsaturated compounds into saturated ones. This reaction is applicable to which of the following compounds? **[INJSO_II-2013]**

(A) Ethyl alcohol (B) Chloroethane (C) Vegetable oils (D) Animal fat

Q.10 One of the test used to distinguish a saturated from an unsaturated compound is bromine water test. Ethene and ethane are reacted with bromine water and the results are displayed on the table given below. From the following table choose the correct observation. **[INJSO_II-2013]**

Ethene **Ethane**

(A)
$$\begin{array}{ccccccc} & & Br & & Br & & \\ & & | & & | & & \\ H & - & C & - & C & - & H \\ & & | & & | & & \\ & & H & & H & & \end{array} \text{(with decolourisation)} \qquad \begin{array}{ccccccc} & & Br & & Br & & \\ & & | & & | & & \\ Br & - & C & - & C & - & H \\ & & | & & | & & \\ & & H & & H & & \end{array} \text{(with decolourisation)}$$

(B)
$$\begin{array}{ccccccc} & & Br & & H & & \\ & & | & & | & & \\ Br & - & C & - & C & - & H \\ & & | & & | & & \\ & & H & & H & & \end{array} \text{(with no decolourisation)} \qquad \begin{array}{ccccccc} & & Br & & Br & & \\ & & | & & | & & \\ H & - & C & - & C & - & H \\ & & | & & | & & \\ & & H & & H & & \end{array} \text{(with no decolourisation)}$$

(C)
$$\begin{array}{ccccccc} & & Br & & Br & & \\ & & | & & | & & \\ H & - & C & - & C & - & H \\ & & | & & | & & \\ & & H & & H & & \end{array} \text{(with decolourisation)}$$
No reaction.

(D) No reaction
$$\begin{array}{ccccccc} & & Br & & Br & & \\ & & | & & | & & \\ Br & - & C & - & C & - & Br \\ & & | & & | & & \\ & & H & & H & & \end{array} \text{(with no decolourisation)}$$

Q.11 Formula of Freon-11 is : **[NTSE-I-2006]**

(A) CCl_3F (B) CCl_2F_2 (C) $CCl_3\,CCl_2F$ (D) $CCl_2F{\cdot}CCl_2F$

Q.12 Barely is ground to powder, then powder is mixed with water and some yeast. The mixture is kept in a closed and moist container, which of the following is produced? **[NTSE-II 2011]**

(A) Sodium bicarbonate (B) Alcohal only

(C) Carbon dioxide only (D) Alcohal and carbon dioxide

Q.13 A hydrocarbon has a molecular formula as C_6H_{12}. It does not react with hydrogen to give C_6H_{14} nor does it react with chlorine to give $C_6H_{12}Cl_2$. The hydrocarbon C_6H_{12} is - **[NTSE-II 2014]**

(i) A saturated hydrocarbon (ii) An unsaturated hydrocarbon

(iii) An open chain hydrocarbon (iv) A cyclo-alkane

(A) (i) and (ii) (B) (iii) and (iv) (C) (ii) and (iv) (D) (i) and (iv)

Q.14 An organic compound is a clear liquid having a molecular formula C_4H_{80}. It has an open chain structure without and carbon - carbon double bond. the compound can be- **[NTSE-II 2014]**
(a) an alcohol (b) an ester (c) an aldehyde (d) a ketone
(A) (a) and (b) (B) (c) and (d) (C) (b) and (d) (D) (d) and (a)

Q.15 IUPAC name of the first member of homologous series of ketones is **[NTSE-I-2015]**
(A) Ethanone (B) Propanol (C) Methanone (D) Propanone

Q.16 An alkyne has 4 numbers of hydrogen atoms. What will be the number of carbon atoms in it ?
(A) Two (B) Three (C) Four (D) Five **[NTSE-I-2015]**

Q.17 The molecular formula of carboxylic acid that differs from rest is - **[NTSE-II 2016]**
(A) $C_{13}H_{26}O_2$ (B) $C_2H_4O_2$ (C) $C_9H_{18}O_2$ (D) $C_7H_{12}O_2$

Q.18 Foam of soap always apper is white as - **[NTSE-II 2016]**
(A) It contains large hydrocarbon chains.
(B) It absorbs red portion of visible light.
(C) It reflects light of all wavelength.
(D) It has one hydrophobic end which is insoluble in water.

Q.19 Unsaturated fatty acids contain - **[NSTSE-11]**
(A) atleast one double bond (B) two double bonds
(C) more than two double bonds (D) no double

Q.20 Which statement about an homologous series is incorrect? **[NSTSE-12]**
(A) All the members of the series have similar chemical reactions.
(B) All the members of the series have the same functional group.
(C) All the members of the series have the same general formula
(D) All the members of the series have similar physical properties.

Q.21 The gases X and Y, have the following properties. **[NSTSE-12]**
- X dissolves in aqueous sodium.
- Y burns in excess oxygen to give X and water only.
- Y does not decolourise aqueous bromine.
What are gases X and Y?

	X	**Y**
(A)	Carbon monoxide	ethane
(B)	Carbon monoxide	ethane
(C)	Carbon dioxide	ethane
(D)	Carbon dioxide	ethane

Q.22 One mole of hydrocarbon X reacted completely with one mole of hydrogen gas in the presence of a heated catalyst. What could be the formula of X? **[NSTSE-12]**
(A) C_2H_6 (B) C_4H_{10} (C) C_5H_{10} (D) C_7H_{16}

Q.23 The structures of four organic compounds are shown below: **[NSTSE-12]**

H | H – C – C(=O)–O–H | H (1)	H, H \> C = C \< H, O–H (2)
H H H | | | H – C – C – C – H | | | H H H (3)	H H | | H – C – C = C \< H, H | H (4)

Which compounds decolourise bromine water?

(A) 1 and 2 only (B) 1, 2 and 4 only (C) 2 and 4 only (D) 3 and 4 only

Q.24 Which of the following can be used to distinguish between ethene and ethane? **[NSTSE-13]**

(A) A lighted splinter (B) Aqueous bromine

(C) Litmus solution (D) Lime water

Q.25 Study the list of compounds given **[NSTSE-13]**

C_2H_2

C_3H_4

C_4H_6

C_5H_8

C_6H_{10}

What do all the members of the given compounds have in common?

(A) The empirical formula (B) The general formula

(C) The molecular formula (D) The structure

Q.26 The IUPAC name of the given hydrocarbon is : **[IOS-13]**

```
          H
          |
      H – C – H
          |
     H    |    H
     |    |    |
 H – C – C – C – H
     |    |    |
     H    H    H
```

(A) n-pentane (B) Isobutane (C) Hexyne (D) n-hexane

Q.27 Which of the following is the molecular formula of propane? **[IOS-13]**

(A) C_3H_6 (B) C_3H_3 (C) C_3H_{12} (D) C_3H_8

Q.28 In the reaction. **[KVPY - Part - II/ 2007]**

Glucose $\xrightarrow{\text{yeast}}$ X $\xrightarrow{KMnO_4}$ Y

the products X and Y respectively are

(A) EtOH, CH_3COOH (B) MeOH, HCOOH

(C) EtOH, CH_2CHO (D) EtOH, $OHCH_2CH_2OH$

Q.29 Among butane, 1-butanol and butanal, the compound which is most polar is : **[KVPY - Part - I/ 2008]**

(A) Butane (B) 1-Butene (C) 1-Butanol (D) Butanal

Q.30 Among ethanol, dimethyl ether, methanol, and propanol, the isomers are : **[KVPY - Part - I/ 2008]**

(A) ethanol, dimethyl ether, methanol and propanol.

(B) ethanol and methanol

(C) ethanol, dimethyl ether and methanol

(D) ethanol and dimethyl ether

Q.31 Esterification of a compound X with molecular formula $C_3H_6O_2$ with an alcohol Y produces a compound with molecular formula $C_5H_{10}O_2$ X and Y, respectively are : **[KVPY - Part - II/ 2008]**

(A) propanoic acid and methanol (B) propanoic acid and ethanol

(C) acetic acid and ethanol (D) butyric acid and methanol

Q.32 When calcium carbide is added to water, the gas that is evolved is : **[KVPY - Part - I/ 2009]**

(A) carbon dioxide (B) hydrogen (C) acetylene (D) methane

Q.33 Ehtanol on reaction with alkaline $KMnO_4$ gives X which when reacted with methanol in the presence of an acid gives a sweet smelling compound Y, X and Y respectively are : **[KVPY - Part - II/ 2009]**

(A) acetaldehyde and acetone (B) acetic acid and methyl acetate

(C) formic acid and methyl formate (D) ethylene and ethyl methyl ether

Q.34 Which is wrong IUPAC name ? **[AIEEE 2002]**

(A) $CH_3CH_2CH_2COOCH_2CH_3$ (Ethyl butanoate)

(B) $CH_3\underset{\displaystyle CH_2}{\underset{|}{C}}HCH_2CHO$ (3-Methyl butanol)

(C) $CH_3\underset{\displaystyle OH}{\underset{|}{C}}H\underset{\displaystyle CH_3}{\underset{|}{C}}HCH_2$ (2-Methyl-3-butanol)

(D) $CH_3\underset{\displaystyle CH_3}{\underset{|}{C}}HCOCH_2CH_3$ (2-Methyl-3-petanone)

Q.35 The IUPAC name of is - **[AIEEE 2007]**

(A) 1,1-diethyl-2,3-dimethyl pentane
(B) 4,4-dimethyl-5,5-dimethyl pentane
(C) 5,5-diethyl-4, 4-dimethyl pentane
(D) 3-ethyl-4, 4-dimethyl heptane

Q.36 The compound which has one isopropyl group is - **[IIT 1987]**
(A) 2,2,3,3-Tetramethylpentane
(B) 2,2-Dimethylpentane
(C) 2,2,3-Trimethylpentane
(D) 2-Methylpentane

Q.37 The correct IUPAC name of the compound **[IIT 1990]**

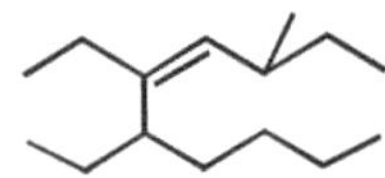

(A) 5, 6-diethyl-8-methyldee-6-ene
(B) 6-Butyl-5-ethyl-3-methyloct-4-ene
(C) 5,6-Diethyl-3-methyl-4-ene
(D) 2,4,5-Triethylnon-3-ene

Q.38 Match the column I with column II and mark the appropriate option given below:

Column I	**Column II**
(a) $C_2H_5OH \rightarrow CH_3COOH$	(i) conc. H_2SO_4 , 170°C
(b) $C_2H_5OH \rightarrow CH_2 = CH_2$	(ii) H_2, Ni
(c) $CH_4 \rightarrow CH_3Cl$	(iii) Alkaline $KMnO_4$
(d) $CH_2 = CH_2 \rightarrow CH_3CH_2$	(iv) Cl_2, Sunlight

(A) (a) - (i), (b) - (iii), (c)- (ii), (d) -(iv)
(B) (a) - (iv), (b) - (iii), (c)- (ii), (d) -(i)
(C) (a) - (i), (b) - (iv), (c)- (iii), (d) -(ii)
(D) (a) - (iii), (b) - (i), (c)- (iv), (d) -(ii)

Q.39 Which of the following general formulae represents the alkyl group?
(A) C_nH_{2n} (B) C_nH_{2n-1} (C) C_nH_{2n+2} (D) C_nH_{2n-1}

Q.40 Rasika mixed sugarcane juice with yeast and kept in covered and sealed pot for a few days. After opening the pot she noticed that the juice started giving a strong smell. She filtered the juice and filled it in the bottles. What is the name of the process and what is the product formed?
(A) Fermentation, Ethyl alcohol
(B) Decomposition, Glucose
(C) Esterification, Fructose
(D) Fermentation, Acetic acid

Q.41 An organic compound X with molecular formula C_2H_6O on oxidation with potassium dichromate and sulphuric acid gives an acidic compound Y. The compounds X and Y react on warming in presence of conc. H_2SO_4 to give a sweet smelling compound Z. What are X, Y and Z?

	X	**Y**	**Z**
(A)	C_2H_5OH	CH_3COOH	$CH_3COOC_2H_5$
(B)	C_2H_5OH	$HCOOH$	$HCOOC_2H_5$
(C)	C_2H_5OH	C_2H_5COOH	$C_2H_5COOC_2H_5$
(D)	C_2H_5OH	CH_3COOH	CH_3COOCH_3

ANSWER KEY

CONCEPT APPLICATION LEVEL - II

SECTION-A

Q.1	C	Q.2	C	Q.3	D	Q.4	B	Q.5	C	Q.6	B	Q.7	B
Q.8	C	Q.9	D	Q.10	A	Q.11	A						

CONCEPT APPLICATION LEVEL - III

Q.1	B	Q.2	D	Q.3	D	Q.4	C	Q.5	D	Q.6	C	Q.7	B
Q.8	B	Q.9	C	Q.10	C	Q.11	A	Q.12	D	Q.13	D	Q.14	B
Q.15	D	Q.16	B	Q.17	D	Q.18	C	Q.19	B	Q.20	D	Q.21	C
Q.22	C	Q.23	C	Q.24	A	Q.25	B	Q.26	B	Q.27	D	Q.28	A
Q.29	C	Q.30	D	Q.31	B	Q.32	C	Q.33	B	Q.34	C	Q.35	D
Q.36	D	Q.37	C	Q.38	D	Q.39	D	Q.40	A	Q.41	A		

5 PERIODIC CLASSIFICATION

5.1 INTRODUCTION :

At present 118 elements are known to us. Around the year 1800, only 30 elements were known. All these had seemingly different properties.

As different elements were being discovered, scientists gathered more and more information about the properties of these elements. They found it difficult to organise all that was known about the elements. They started looking for some pattern in their properties. On the basis of which they could study such a large number of elements with ease.

5.2 WHY DO WE NEED TO CLASSIFY ELEMENTS ?

Before the begining of eighteenth century, only a very few elements were known and it was quite easy to study and remember their individual properties. However, the situation became difficult with the discovery of large number of elements in the later years. At this stage the scientists felt the need of some simple method to facilitate the study of the properties of various elements and their compounds. After numerous attempts the scientists were ultimately successful in arranging the elements in such a way so that similar elements were grouped together and different elements were separated.

5.3 MAKING ORDER OUT OF CHAOS-EARLY ATTEMPT AT THE CLASSIFICATION OF ELEMENTS :

5.3.1 Dobereiners triads

In 1817, J.W. Dobereiner, a german scientist gave this arrangement of elements.

(i) He made groups of three elements having similar chemical properties called **TRIAD**.

(ii) In Dobereiner triad, atomic weight. of middle element is equal to the average atomic weight of first and third element.

Example :

Triad	Li	Na	K
Relative Atomic Mass	7	23	39

$\frac{7+39}{2} = 23$

Dobereiner's Triads :

Triad	Relative atomic masses respectively	Arithmetic mean of atomic masses of first and the third elements.
S, Se, Te	32, 79, 128	$\frac{32+128}{2} = 80$
Cl, Br, I	35.5, 80, 127	$\frac{35.5+127}{2} = 81.25$
Ca, Sr, Ba	40, 88, 137	$\frac{40+137}{2} = 88.5$

5.3.2 Limitations

Dobereiner could identify only three triads from the elements known at that time. hence this system of classification into triads was not found to be useful for classifying many other elements which were not able to form any traids like all three previous triads.

Illustration 1

The law of triad is applicable to

(A) C, N, O (B) H, O, N (C) Na, K, Rb (D) Cl, Br, I

Solution

(D) Cl, Br, I

Illustration 2

The law of triad is not applicable to

(A) Cl, Br, I (B) Na, K, Rb (C) S, Se, Te (D) Ca, Sr, Ba

Solution

(B) Na, K, Rb

Illustration 3

X, Y, Z are three members of a Dobereiner's triad. The atomic mass of X is 7 μ and that of Y is 23 μ. What is the atomic mass of Z?

Solution

The triads is X, Y, Z. Let the atomic mass of Z be x, then according to Dobereiner.

$$\text{Atomic mass of Y} = \frac{\text{Atomic mass of X} + \text{Atomic mass of Z}}{2}$$

$$23\ \mu = \frac{7\mu + x}{2}$$

$$x = 2 \times 23\ \mu - 7\mu = 46\ \mu - 7\ \mu = 39\ \mu$$

Therefore, the atomic mass of Z is 39 μ.

5.4 NEWLAND LAW OF OCTAVES (1865):

In 1864, John Alexander Newland, an English chemist noticed that "when elements are arranged in the increasing order of their atomic masses every eighth element had properties similar to first element".

(i) He arranged the elements in the increasing order of their atomic mass and observe that properties of every 8th element was similar to the 1st one. Like in the case of musical vowels notation.

Sa	Re	Ga	Ma	Pa	Dha	Ne	Sa
1	2	3	4	5	6	7	8

(ii) At that time inert gases were not known.

Sa (do)	re (re)	ga (mi)	ma (fa)	pa (so)	da (la)	ni (ti)
H	**Li**	**Be**	B	C	N	O
F	**Na**	**Mg**	Al	Si	P	S
Cl	K	Ca	Cr	Ti	Mn	Fe
Co and Ni	Cu	Zn	Y	In	As	Se
Br	Rb	Sr	Ce and Na	Zr	–	–

(iii) The properties of Li are similar to 8th element i.e. Na, Be are similar to Mg and so on.

Drawback or Limitation :

- It was found that the **law of octaves** was applicable only upto calcium, as after calcium every eighth element did not possess properties similar to that of the first.
- It was assumed by **Newlands** that only 56 elements existed in nature and no more elements would be discovered in future. But later on several new elements were discovered whose properties did not fit Newland's law of Octaves.
- In order to fit elements into his table, Newland adjusted two elements in the same slot, but also put some unlike elements under the same note. Can you find examples of these from Table? Note that cobalt and nickel are in the same slot and these are placed in the same column as fluorine, chlorine and bromine which have very different properties than these elements, Iron, which resembles cobalt and nickel in properties has been placed far away from these elements.

Thus, Newland's law of Octaves worked well with lighter elements only

5.5 LOTHER MEYER'S CURVE (1869):

(i) He plotted a curve between atomic weight and atomic volume of different elements.

(ii) The following observation can be made from the curve-

(a) Most electropositive elements i.e. Alkali metals (Li, Na, K, Rb, Cs etc.) occupy the peak positions on the curve.

(b) Less electropositive i.e. Alkaline earth metal (Be, Mg, Ca, Sr, Ba) occupy the descending position on the curve.

(c) Metalloids (B, Si, Te, At etc) and transition metals occupy bottom part of the curve.

(d) Most electronegative i.e. halogens (F, Cl, Br, I) occupy the ascending position on the curve.

Note : Elements having similar properties occupy similar position on the curve.

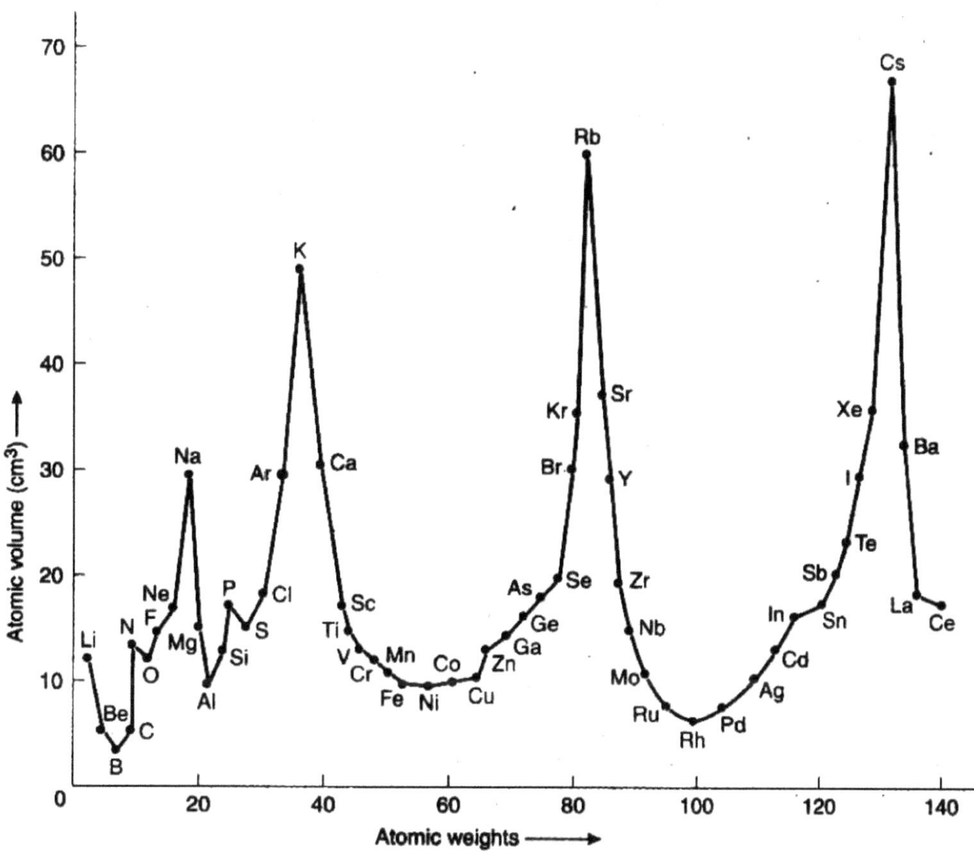

Conclusion :

On the basis of the curve **Lother Meyer** proposed that the physical properties of the elements are periodic function of their atomic wt. and this become the base of **Mendeleev's periodic table**.

Illustration 4

What is periodic function.

Solution

The periodic function is a function that repeats it value (physical and chemical properties) in regular interval or periods. .

5.6 MENDELEEV'S PERIODIC TABLE (1869) :

Mendeleev's Periodic Table was published in a German journal in 1872. In the formula for oxides and hydrides at the top of the columns, the letter R is used to represent any of the elements in the group. Note the way formulae are written. For example, the hydride of carbon, CH_4 is written as RH_4 and the oxide CO_2 as RO_2.

Group	I		II		III		IV		V		VI		VII		VIII
Oxide Hydride	R_2O RH		RO RH_2		R_2O_3 RH_3		RO_2 RH_4		R_2O_5 RH_3		RO_3 RH_2		R_2O_7 RH		RO_4
Periods ↓	A	B	A	B	A	B	A	B	A	B	A	B	A	B	Transition Series
1	H 1.008														
2	Li 6.939		Be 9.012		B 10.81		C 12.011		N 14.007		O 15.999		F 18.998		
3	Na 22.99		Mg 24.31		Al 29.98		Si 28.09		P 30.974		S 32.06		Cl 35.453		
4 First series	K 39.102		Ca 40.08			Sc 44.96		Ti 47.90		V 50.94		Cr 50.20		Mn 54.94	Fe 55.85 Co 58.93 Ni 58.71
Second series		Cu 63.54		Zn 65.37	Ga 69.72		Ge 72.59		As 74.92		Se 78.96		Br 79.909		
5 First series	Rb 85.47		Sr 87.62			Y 88.91		Zr 91.22		Nb 92.91		Mo 95.94		Tc 99	Ru 101.07 Co 102.91 Ni 106.4
Second series		Ag 107.87		Cd 112.40	In 114.82		Sn 118.69		Sb 121.75		Te 127.60		I 126.90		
6 First series	Cs 132.90		Ba 137.34			La 138.91		Hf 178.49		Ta 180.95		W 183.85			Os 190.2 Ir 192.2 Pt 195.09
Second series		Au 196.97		Hg 200.59	Tl 204.37		Pb 207.19		Bi 208.98						

(i) **Mendeleev's Periodic Law** : The physical and chemical properties of elements are the periodic function of their atomic weight.

(ii) **Characteristic of Mendeleev's periodic table.**

(a) It was based on atomic weight.

(b) 63 elements were known at that time.

(c) Noble gases were not discovered.

(d) He was the first scientist to classify the elements in a systematic manner i.e. in horizontal rows and in vertical columns.

(e) Horizontal rows are called periods and there were 7 periods in Mendeleev's periodic table.

(f) Vertical columns are called groups and there were 8 groups in Mendeleev's Periodic table.

(g) Each group upto VII is divided into A & B subgroups, 'A' sub groups elements are called normal elements and 'B' subgroups elements are called transition elements.

(h) The VIII group contains 9 elements in three rows (Transitional metals group)

(i) The elements belonging to same group exhibit similar properties.

5.6.1 Achievements of Mendeleev's Periodic Table

(i) **Predication of undiscovered element :** Further, Mendeleev left some gaps in his Periodic Table. Instead of looking upon these gaps as defects, Mendeleev predicted the existence of some elements that had not been discovered at that time.

Mendeleev named them by prefixing a Sanskrit numeral, Eka (one) to the name of preceding element in the same group.

For instance, scandium, gallium and germanium, discovered later, have properties similar to B, Al, Si that's why they were termed as Eka-boron, Eka-aluminium and Eka-silicon respectively. The properties of Eka-aluminium predicted by Mendeleev and those of the element, gallium which was discovered later and replaced Eka-aluminium are listed as follows

Table: Properties of Eka-aluminium and gallium

Property	Preducted properties of Eka-alumnium	Real properties of Gallium
Atomic mass	68	69.7
Formula of Oxide	E_2O_3	Ga_2O_3
Formula of Chloride	ECl_3	$GaCl_3$

(ii) Classification of elements : This provided convincing evidence for both the correctness and usefulness of Mendeleev's Periodic Table. Further, it was the extraordinary success of Mendeleev's prediction that led chemists not only to accept his Periodic Table but also recognise him, as the originator of the concept on which it based. Mendeleev's periodic table could perdict the properties of several elements on the basis of their position in the periodic table.

(iii) Correction of doubtful atomic weights of some elements : Initially Berilium assumed as trivalent and equivalent weight = 4.5

Atomic Weight = Valency × equivalent weight

= 3 × 4.5

= 13.5

But there is no space for such element then correction has been done and Berilium assumed as divalent.

Atomic Weight = Valency × equivalent weight

= 2 × 4.5

= 9

Other example, Atomic weight correction are U, Be, Ln, Au, Pt.

5.6.2 Limitations of Mendeleev's Classification

1. **Anomalous pairs of elements :** While developing the Periodic Table, there were a few instances where Mendeleev had to place an element with a slightly greater atomic mass before an element with a slightly lower atomic mass. The sequence was inverted so that elements with similar properties could be grouped together. For example, cobalt (atomic mass 58.9) appeared before nickel (atomic mass 58.7).
2. **Position of Hydrogen :** Electronic configuration of **hydrogen** resembles that of **alkali metals**. Like alkali metals, hydrogen combines with halogens, oxygen and sulphur to form compounds having similar formulae.
   On the other hand, just like halogens, hydrogen also exists as diatomic molecules and it combines with metals and non-metals to form covalent compounds.
3. **Position of Isotopes:** Isotopes of elements were placed in the same position in the table though according to their atomic weights, they should have been placed in different position.

4. **Separation of similar but grouping of certain dissimilar elements:** Certain chemically similar elements like copper and mercury were placed in different group while some other dissimilar elements like copper, silver and gold have been placed in the same group.

5. **Noble gases** like helium (He), neon (Ne) and argon (Ar) have been discovered later because they are very inert and present in extremely low concentrations in our atmosphere. One of the strengths of Mendeleev's Periodic Table was that, when these gases were discovered, they could be placed in a new group without disturbing the existing order.

6. **Lanthanides and Actinides:** A group of 14 elements (at No. 58 to 71) called rare earths metal or lanthanide were placed together in one position i.e. in group III B of 6th period. Similarly another group of elements called actinides do not find their proper places in this periodic table.

Illustrations

Illustration 5

Many scientists before Mendeleev also used atomic mass as the basis of classification, but why did only Mendeleev succeed.

Solution

The secret of Mendeleev's success was that although the classification was based on atomic mass, but at many places he did not follow this rule rigidly. He laid major stress on the similarity in the chemical and physical properties.

Illustration 6

Why did Mendeleev leave many gaps in his periodic table?

Solution

Mendeleev predicted that there were many elements yet to be discovered. So, when none of the elements known at that time fit into a particular position, he left a gap there. Later, when more elements were discovered these were found to fit into these gaps.

5.7 MAKING ORDER OUT OF CHOAS-THE MODERN PERIODIC TABLE :

A large number of scientists made attempts to remove drawbacks of Mendeleev's periodic table. In 1913, the English Physicist Henry Moseley studied the X-ray spectra of many elements. He observed that a plot $\sqrt{v}$ (where v is the frequency of the X-rays emitted) against atomic number (Z) gave a straight line and not the plot of $\sqrt{v}$ against atomic weight. He proposed that atomic number is a more fundamental property of an element than its atomic weight. Therefore, the physical and chemical properties of the elements are determined by their atomic numbers instead of their atomic weights. This observation led to the development of modern periodic law and the **modern periodic law** can be stated as follows:

Properties of elements are a periodic function of their atomic number.

Let us recall that the atomic number gives us the number of protons in the nucleus of an atom and this number increases by one in going from one element to the next. Elements, when arranged in order of increasing atomic number Z, lead us to the classification known as the **modern periodic table.** Prediction of properties of elements could be made with more precision when elements were arranged on the basis of increasing atomic number.

5.7.1 What is Periodicity

The recurrence of properties of the elements, after a certain regular intervals, when they are arranged in the increasing order of their atomic numbers, is called **periodicity.**

5.7.2 Cause of Periodicity

We know that properties of elements depend upon the number of valence electrons, i.e. the number of electrons in the outermost shell. When the elements are arranged in the increasing order of their atomic numbers, then the elements having the same numbers of valence electrons are repeated at regular intervals of 2, 8, 8, 18, 18, 32....... Since the chemical properties depend upon the number of valence electrons, therefore, chemical properties are repeated at regular intervals, i.e. there is periodicity in the chemical properties of the elements.

Periodic table of the elements

- alkali metals
- alkaline earth metals
- transition metals
- other metals
- other nonmetals
- halogens
- noble gases
- rare earth elements (21, 39, 57–71) lanthanide elements (57–71 only)
- actinide elements

period \ group	1* Ia**	2 IIa	3 IIIb	4 IVb	5 Vb	6 VIb	7 VIIb	8 VIIIb	9 VIIIb	10 VIIIb	11 Ib	12 IIb	13 IIIa	14 IVa	15 Va	16 VIa	17 VIIa	18 0
1	1 H																	2 He
2	3 Li	4 Be											5 B	6 C	7 N	8 O	9 F	10 Ne
3	11 Na	12 Mg											13 Al	14 Si	15 P	16 S	17 Cl	18 Ar
4	19 K	20 Ca	21 Sc	22 Ti	23 V	24 Cr	25 Mn	26 Fe	27 Co	28 Ni	29 Cu	30 Zn	31 Ga	32 Ge	33 As	34 Se	35 Br	36 Kr
5	37 Rb	38 Sr	39 Y	40 Zr	41 Nb	42 Mo	43 Tc	44 Ru	45 Rh	46 Pd	47 Ag	48 Cd	49 In	50 Sn	51 Sb	52 Te	53 I	54 Xe
6	55 Cs	56 Ba	57 La	72 Hf	73 Ta	74 W	75 Re	76 Os	77 Ir	78 Pt	79 Au	80 Hg	81 Tl	82 Pb	83 Bi	84 Po	85 At	86 Rn
7	87 Fr	88 Ra	89 Ac	104 Rf	105 Db	106 Sg	107 Bh	108 Hs	109 Mt	110 Ds	111 Rg	112 *** (Uub)	113 *** (Uut)	114 *** (Uuq)	115 *** (Uup)	116 *** (Uuh)		

lanthanide series 6	58 Ce	59 Pr	60 Nd	61 Pm	62 Sm	63 Eu	64 Gd	65 Tb	66 Dy	67 Ho	68 Er	69 Tm	70 Yb	71 Lu
actinide series 7	90 Th	91 Pa	92 U	93 Np	94 Pu	95 Am	96 Cm	97 Bk	98 Cf	99 Es	100 Fm	101 Md	102 No	103 Lr

* Numbering system adopted by the International Union of Pure and Applied Chemistry (IUPAC).
** Numbering system widely used, especially in the U.S., from the mid-20th century.
*** Discoveries of elements 112–116 are claimed but not confirmed. Element names and symbols in parentheses are temporarily assigned by IUPAC.

5.7.3 Long form of periodic table :

Groups:- The 18 vertical columns are called groups. The elements belonging to a particular group is known as a family and is usually named after the first number. Apart from this some of the groups are given typical name as examplified beneath.

(i) Elements of group 1 are called **ALKALI METALS .**

(ii) Elements of group 2 are called **ALKALINE EARTH METALS.**

(iii) Elements of group 15 are called **PNICTOGENS.** Means choking to system due to toxicity.

(iv) Elements of group 16 are called **CHALCOGENS.**

(v) Elements of group 17 are called **HALOGENS.**

(vi) Elements of group 18 are called **NOBLE GASES OR AEROGENS.**

All the other groups are named after the first member of each group.

A few important characteristics of the elements present in groups are listed.

(i) The elements present in a group are separated by definite gaps of atomic numbers (8, 8, 18, 18, 32). These are called magic numbers.

(ii) There are eighteen (18) independent groups in the Long from of Periodic Table. These are numbered from 1 to 18.

(iii) The elements present in a group have the same number of electrons in the valence shell of their atoms.

(iv) The elements present in a group have the same valency.

(v) The elements present in group have identical chemical properties.

(vi) The physical properties of the elements in group such as melting point, boiling point, density vary gradually.

(vii) Atomic radii of the elements present in a group increase downwards.

Periods : The horizontal rows are called periods. There are Seven Periods in the long form of the periodic Table.

Period	n	Subshell	No.of Element	Element	Name of Period
1	1	1s	2	1H – 2He	Shortest
2	2	2s, 2p	8	3Li – 10Ne	Short
3	3	3s, 3p	8	11Na – 18Ar	Short
4	4	4s, 3d, 4p	18	19K – 36Kr	Long
5	5	5s, 4d, 5p	18	37Rb – 58Xe	Long
6	6	6s, 4f, 5d, 6p,	32	55Cs – 86Rn	Longest
7	7	7s, 5f, 6d	26	87Fr – 112UUb	Incomplete

The important characteristics of the elements in a period are as follows :

(i) In all the elements present in a period the electrons are filled in the valence shell.

(ii) As the number of electrons in the valence shell change, the chemical properties of the elements present in a period also change.

(iii) Atomic radii of the elements in a period decrease from left to the right.

(iv) Along a period, the metallic character of the elements decreases and the non-metallic character increases.

(v) Along a period, the reducing character of the elements decreases and their oxidizing character increases.

Both the lanthanide and actinide series of elements were placed under the rest of the periodic table. These elements technically should be placed between the alkaline earth metals and the transition metals, however, since this would make the periodic table too wide, they were placed below the rest of the elements.

5.7.4 DIVISION OF THE PERIODIC TABLE IN s, p, d and f blocks :

The periodic table is divided into four main blocks (s, p, d and f) depending upon the subshell to which the valence electron enters into.

(i) Elements of group 1 and 2 constitute s-block.

(ii) Elements of group 13, 14, 15, 16, 17, 18 constitute p-block.

(iii) Elements of groups 3, 4, 5, 6, 7, 8, 9, 10, 11, 12 constitute d-block.

(iv) The f-block element comprise two horizontal rows placed at the bottom of the periodic table to avoid its unnecessary expansion.

Elements of s and p-block are called normal or representative elements, those of d-block are called transition elements while the f-block elements are called inner transition elements.

s-Blocks Elements :

The elements in which the last electron enters the s-sub-shell of their outermost energy level and electronic configuration is ns^1 *or* ns^2 *(I or II group) are called* **s-block elements are :**

(i) They are soft metals.

(ii) They have low ionisation energies.

(ii) They are very reactive and form ionic compounds.

(iv) They show oxidation states of +1 group and +2 group.

(v) They are good reducing agents.

(vi) They form basic oxide.

***p*- Block Elements :**

The elements in which the last electron enters the p-sub-shell of their outermost energy level are called **p-block elements.** The exception is helium ($1s^2$).

The general configuration of their outermost shell is $\mathbf{ns^2\ np^{1\text{-}6}}$**.** These elements are kept in group 13 to 18. Some of the general characteristics of p-block elements are:

(i) They show variable oxidation states.

(ii) They form ionic as well as covalent compounds.

(iii) Most of them are non-metals.

(iv) Most of them form acidic oxides.

***d*- Block Elements :**

(i) They are hard and having high melting point.

(ii) They show variable oxidation states.

(iii) They form coloured complexes.

(iv) They form ionic as well as covalent compounds.

(v) Most of them exhibit paramagnetism.

(vi) Most of them possess catalytic properties.

f- Block Elements :

The elements in which the last electron enters the ***f*- block elements.**

Their general configuration is $(n-2)f^{1-14}(n-1)d^{0-1}ns^2$. They consist of two series of 28 elements (14 in each) placed at the bottom of the periodic table.

The elements of first series followed by lanthanum ($_{57}$La) are called **Lanthanides**.

The elements of second series followed by actinium ($_{89}$Ac) are called **Actinides**.

The general **Characterstics of *f*-block elements are :**

(i) They show variable oxidation states.

(ii) They have high melting points.

(iii) They have high densities.

(iv) They form coloured compounds.

(v) Most of the elements of actinide series are radioactive.

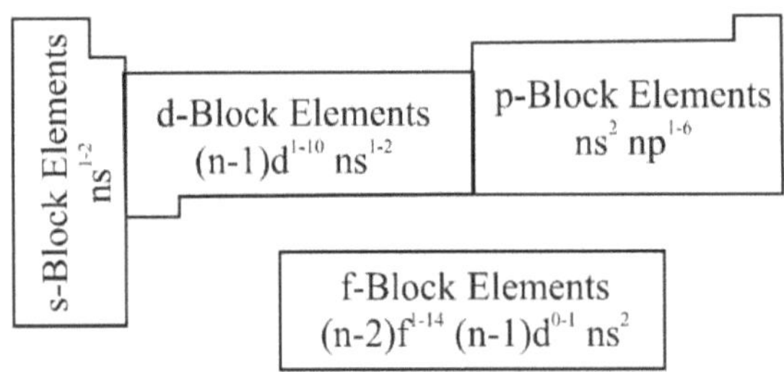

NOTE:

1. The elements of group zero are called ***inert gases, noble gases, rare gases* or *aerogens.***
2. The elements of p-block (except noble gases) are called *representative or main group elements.*

The members of this group of elements have all their occupied subshells filled except their outermost electron shell.

5.8 ADVANTAGES OF LONG FORM OVER MENDELEEV'S PERIDIC TABLE:

There are several advantages of long form of periodic table over Mendeleev's periodic table. Some of these are as follows:

(i) It is based upon atomic number which is a fundamental property instead of atomic mass.

(ii) The elements have been grouped as s,p,d and f-block elements. which helps us to understand the electronic configuration in a better way.

(iii) In the long form of periodic table, the elements are arranged in the increasing order of their atomic numbers, therefore, no separate place is required for isotopes.

(iv) The position of some of the elements which were a misfit on the basis of atomic mass is now explained on the basis of increase in atomic number. For example, argon proceeds potassium because argon has atomic number 18 which is less than that of potassium which is 19.

(v) Metals, non-metals, metalloids, transition elements, lanthanoids and actinoids are now better classified.

5.9 NOMENCLATURE OF ELEMENTS ATOMIC NUMBER ≥ 100:

According to IUPAC following latin word roots are used for naming of elements having atomic number greater than or equal to 100. The latin words for various digits of the atomic number are written together in the order of which makes the atomic number and suffix ium is added at the end.

Digit	0	1	2	3	4	5	6	7	8	9
Latin Word	Nil	Un	Bi	Tri	Quad	Pent	Hex	Sept	Oct	Enn
Abbrevation	n	u	b	t	q	p	h	s	o	e

For example: The element with atomic number 104 named as follows:

1 0 4 suffix

un nil quad + ium = unnilquadium

and assigned symbol ***Unq***.

Note: These IUPAC names given are temporary later on elements assigned permanent names.

5.10 PERIODIC PROPERTIES :

The properties which are directly or indirectly related to their electronic configuration and show gradual change when we move from left to right in a period or from top to bottom in a group are called **periodic properties.**

(a) Atomic volume, atomic size, melting point, boiling point and density are important physical properties which show periodicity.

(b) Some important chemical properties that exhibit periodicity are electronic configuration, ionisation energy, electron affinity, electronegativity, metallic character, nature of oxides, oxidation state and reducting character etc.

(c) Specific heat, refractive index etc. are not periodic properties.

Some trends in Modern Periodc Table

(A) VALENCY

Valency may be defined as combining capacity of an element.

The Valency of an element is usually determined by the number of electrons in the outermost shell of its atoms. This is because the outer electrons are largely responsible for the chemical behaviour as these electron usually participate in chemical bonding.

(i) Variation of valency in a period. On moving from left to right in each short period, the valency of the elements first increases from 1 to 4 and then decreases and becomes 0 (zero). The trend for the elements of third period is shown below in table.

Variation of Valency of Element of Third Period

Element	Na	Mg	Al	Si	P	S	Cl	Ar
Valency	1	2	3	4	3	2	1	0

(ii) Variation of Valency in a Group. On moving down a group, the number of valence electrons remains the same and due to this all the elements in a particular group have the same valency. For example,

All elements of group 1 shows a **valency** of 1
All elements of group 2 shows a **valency** of 2
All elements of group 13 shows a **valency** of 3
All elements of group 14 shows a **valency** of 4
All elements of group 15 shows a **valency** of 3
All elements of group 16 shows a **valency** of 2
All elements of group 17 shows a **valency** of 1
All elements of group 18 shows a **valency** of 0

(B) METALLIC AND NON-METALLIC CHARACTER.

Generally, **Metals** posses 1, 2 or 3 electrons in their respective valence shells and thus have a strong tendency to lose these electrons to form positive ions. Therefore, metals are also called **electropositive elements** and the metallic character is also called **Electropositive Character.**
Non-Metals, on the other hand, generally have 4 to 8 electrons in their respective outermost shells and thus have a tendency to gain electrons to form negative ions. Therefore non-metals are also called **Electronegative elements** and the non metallic character is also called **electronegative character.**
Variation in a period: On moving from left to right in a period, the metallic character decreases while the non-metallic character increases.

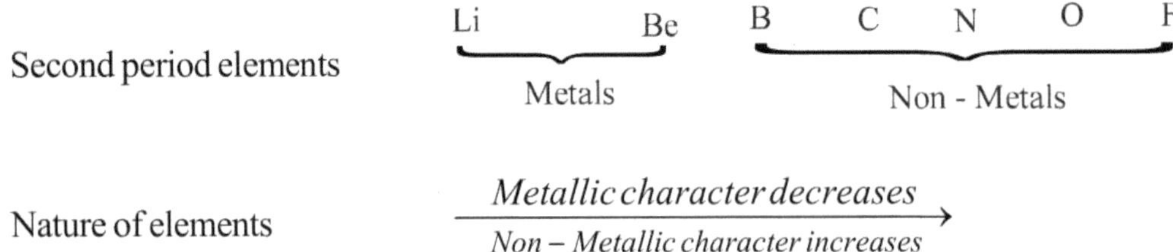

Thus in the second period, lithium is the most metallic element followed by beryllium. The non metallic character starts with boron and keeps on increasing. Thus fluorine is the most non metallic element of the second period.
The change from metallic to non metallic character is more striking among the elements of the third period as shown below :

Third period elements: Na Mg Al (Metals), Si (Metalloid), P S Cl (Non - Metals)

In general, the most metallic element lies on the extreme left hand side while most non metallic element lies on the extreme right hand side of any period.

Variation in a group. On moving down in a group, the metallic character or electropositive character increases.

Elements of Group 1

Element	**Symbol**	**Metallic character**
Lithium	Li	Least metallic element
Sodium	Na	
Potassium	K	Metallic character increases down the group
Rubidium	Rb	
Cesium	Cs	
Francium	Fr	Most metallic element

Conversely, on moving down a group, the non metallic character or electronegative character decreases.

Elements of Group 17

Element	**Symbol**	**Metallic character**
Fluorine	F	Most non metallic element
Chlorine	Cl	
Bromine	Br	Non-Metallic character or electronegative character decreases on moving down the group
Iodine	I	
Astatine	At	Least non-metallic element

Division of elements into Metals and Non-metals: In the long form of the periodic table, the elements have been broadly divided into metals and non metals by the zig-zag line funning diagonally across the periodic table. Those elements which lie on the left hand side of this line are Metals and those which lie on the right hand side of this line are non **metallic**. However, the elements silicon, germanium, arsenicm, antimony and tellurium which lie along the border of this line show the properties of both metals and non metals. These elements are called semi metals or **metalloids**.

The metallic/non metallic character also helps us to predict the nature of oxides formed by the elements. In general, the oxides of metals are basic while those of non metals are acidic in nature. An element behaves as a metal or a non-metal is directly related to its ionization energy. The elements having low values of ionization energies are metals whereas elements having high values of ionization energies are non-metals.

Illustration 7

Elements having atomic number 3 to 18 are shown in the form of a table by using certain letters of the alphabet (These letters are not the usual symbols of these compound)

3 A	4	5	6	7	8	9	10 G
11 B	12 C	13	14 D	15	16	17 F	18

(a) ***Which of these is***

(i) a noble gas ***(ii) a halogen***

(iii) an alkali metal ***(iv) an element with valency 4?***

(b) ***Write the formula of the compound formed when A react with F?***

(c) ***Write the electronic configuration of element G?***

Solution

(a) (i) G (ii) F (iii) A and B (iv) D

(b) $A \rightarrow A^+ + e^-$; $F + e^- \rightarrow F^-$; $A^+ + F^- \rightarrow A^+F^- \rightarrow AF$

So the formula of the compound formed is AF

(c) G has the atomic number 10. So the electronic arrangement in G is 2,8.

(B) ATOMIC RADII

It refers to the distance between the centre of nucleus of atom to its outer most shell of electrons. Since absolute value of atomic size cannot be determined, it is expressed in terms of the operational definitions such as **ionic radius, covalent radius, vander waal's radius and metallic radius.** The absolute value of atomic radius cannot be determined because :

(i) It is not possible to locate the exact position of electrons in an atom as an orbital has no sharp boundaries.

(ii) It is not possible to isolate an individual atom for its size determination.

(iii) In a group of atoms, the probability distribution of electrons is influenced by the presence of neighbouring atoms. Thus, size of an atom may change in going from one environment to other.

However, the value of atomic radii are derived from bond length measured by various techniques such as **X-ray diffraction, electron diffraction, infra-red spectroscopy, nuclear magnetic resonance spectroscopy etc.**

(a) Variation of atomic radii in a period :

Atomic radii (in picometer) of 2nd and 3rd period elements are given in the table given below. In a period, atomic radius generally decreases from left to right with increase in atomic number

2nd period

Li	Be	B	C	N	O	F
152	111	88	77	74	66	42

3rd period

Na	Mg	Al	Si	P	S	Cl
190	145	118	111	98	88	79

In a period there is a gradual increase in the nuclear charge with increase in atomic number. Since valence electrons are added in the same shell and the electron in the same shell do not screen each other from the nucleus, the increase in nuclear charge is not neutralised by the extra valence electron. As a result effective nuclear charge increases therefore valence electrons are more and more strongly attracted towards nucleus. This gradually decrease atomic radii.

Variation of atomic radii in a group :

Atomic radii increases in a group from top to bottom. This can be seen from the data of atomic radii in picometers given for groups 1 and 17 elements below.

Element (group 1)	Atomic Radius	Element (group 2)	Atomic Radius
Li	155	F	72
Na	190	Cl	99
K	235	Br	114
Rb	248	I	133

In moving down the group the nuclear charge increases with increase in atomic number. However, while going down in a group from one atom to another the number of inner shells also increases, although the number of electrons in the outermost shell remains the same. The effect of increase in the size of the electron cloud (due to increase in number of shells) is more pronounced than the effect of increased nuclear charge. Thus, the distance of outermost electron from the nucleus increases as we move down a group. For example, in lithium the valence electron is present in 2nd shell while in sodium it is present in 3rd shell. Also, the number of filled shells between valence electron and nucleus increases. Thus in group 1 Li (2, 1) has one filled shell between its nucleus and valence electron while Na (2, 8, 1) has two filled shells between them. Both the factors decrease the force of attraction between nucleus and valence electron. Therefore atomic size increases on moving down a group.

Factors influencing atomic radius :

(a) **Multiplicity of bond .** Covalent radii depends on the multiplicity of bonds. e.g.

	Bond length	Radius of carbon atom
$H_3C—CH_3$	154 pm	$\frac{154}{2} = 77$ pm
$H_2C = CH_2$	134 pm	$\frac{134}{2} = 67$ pm
$HC \equiv CH$	120 pm	$\frac{120}{2} = 60$ pm

(b) **Percentage of ionic character :** Covalent radius of H in HCl, HBr, and HI are different.

Knowledge Enhancer

(i) **Covalent radius :** It is defined as half of the distance between two successive nuclei of two covalent bonded like atoms in a molecule. If the bond length in between the two atoms is say A-A = d, then

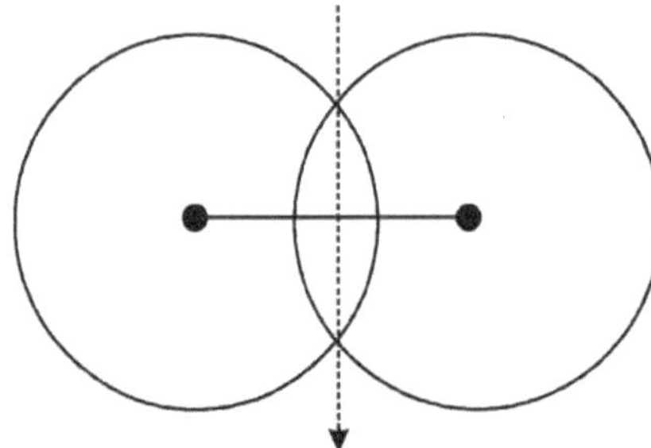

Internuclear distance between two covalently bonded atoms

$$d_{AA} = r_A + r_B$$
$$r_A = d_{\frac{A-A}{2}}$$

Covalent radius (r_{cov}) = ½[Internuclear distance between two covalently bonded like atoms] = ½d

(ii) **Vander Wall's radius ($r_{v,waat}$)** . It is defined as one half of the distance between the nuclei of two non bonded isolated atoms or two adjacent atoms belonging to two neighbouring molecules of an element in the solid state.

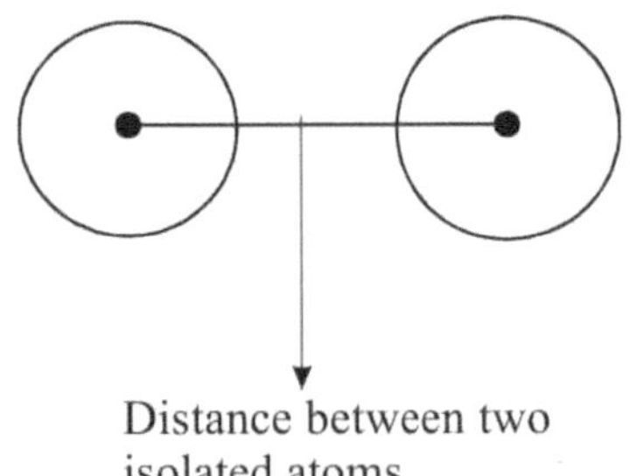

Distance between two isolated atoms

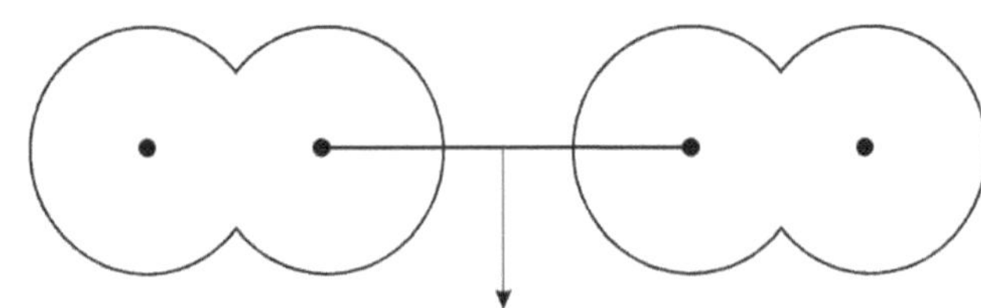

Distance between adjacent atoms belonging to two neighbouring molecules in solid state.

In general, vander waals radius > Covalent radius of an atom.

(iii) **Metallic radius :** It is defined as half the distance between two successive nuclei of two adjacent metal atoms in the metallic closed packed crystal lattice.

(iv) **Ionic Radius :** Ionic radius may be defined as the effective distance from the nucleus of the ion to the point upto which it has an influence in the ionic bond.

When an atom changes into ion, its size changes appreciably.

(a) **The radius of cation is smaller than that of the parent atom.**

(b) **The radius of anion is larger than that of parent atom.**

(c) ***The ions having same number of electrons but different magnitude of nuclear charge are called iso-electronic ions.***

For example, each one of sulphides (S^{2-}), chloride (Cl^{-}), Potassium (K^{+}), and Calcium (Ca^{2+}) ion has eighteen electrons but they have nuclear charge of +16, +17, +19 and +20 respectively.

Within the series of iso-electronic ions, size of the ions decreases with the increase in the magnitude of nuclear charge. For example, N^{3-}, O^{2-}, F^{-}, Na^{+}, Mg^{2+}, Al^{3+} are iso-electronic and have 10 electrons each. The size of these ions are in the order.

$$Al^{3+} < Mg^{2+} < Na^{+} < F^{-} < O^{2-} < N^{3-}$$

NOTE: For isoelectronic Z/e ratio determine atomic radius.

$$\frac{Z}{e} \propto \frac{1}{\text{Atomic Radius}}$$

The ionic radii of these ions are given in Table below :

Ionic Radii of Some Iso-electronic Ions

Atoms	N^{3-}	O^{2-}	F^{-}	Na^{+}	Mg^{2+}	Al^{3+}
Nuclear Charge	+7	+8	+9	+11	+12	+13
Size (pm)	1.71	1.40	1.26	0.95	0.65	0.50

$$\text{Atomic Radius} \propto \frac{1}{\text{Effective Nuclear Charge}}$$

Atomic Radius $\propto$ No. of shell

Atomic Radius $\propto$ Screnning Effect

Atomic Size $\propto$ Magnitude of –ve charge

$$\text{Atomic Size} \propto \frac{1}{\text{Magnitude of positive Charge}}$$

$$\text{Atomic Radius} \propto \frac{1}{\text{Bond Order}}$$

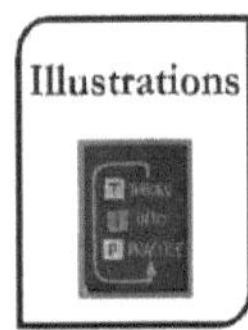

Illustration 8

Give examples of three cations and three anions which are isoelectronic with Argon.

Solution

Cations	:	K^+	Ca^{2+}	Sc^{3+}
Anions	:	Cl^-	S^{2-}	P^{3-}

Illustration 9

A given compound A_2 *has total* d_{A-A} *is 1.4 Å. The atomic (covalent) radius of an atom A is .*

(A) 0.7 Å *(B) 0.5 Å* *(C) 2.8Å* *(D) 7.5 Å*

Solution

$$d_{AA} = r_A + r_B$$
$$r_A = \frac{d_{A-A}}{2}$$

$$r_A = \frac{1.4}{2} = 0.7$$

Illustration 10

The following species are isoelectronic with the noble gas neon. Arrange them in order of increasing size : Na^+, F^-, O^{2-}, Mg^{2+}, Al^{3+}.

Solution

In Na^+, F^-, O^{2-}, Mg^{2+}, Al^{3+}, the nuclear charges are 11, 9, 8, 12 and 13 respectively. Among isoelectronic species, greater the nuclear charge smaller is the size. Therefore, the sizes of the above ionic species are in the order :

$$\mathbf{Al^{3+} < Mg^{2+} < Na^+ < F^- < O^{2-}.}$$

Illustration 11

Out of Na^+ and Na which has smaller size and why?

Solution

Na^+ has smaller size than Na : Na^+ has one electron less than Na. However, Na and Na^+ have same nuclear charge. Therefore, electrons in Na^+ are more tighty held than in Na. So, removal of one electron from Na leads to complete removal of the third shell so that in Na^+, the outermost shell is second. Hence, Na^+ has smaller size than Na.

(C) IONISATION ENERGY / IONISATION POTENTIAL

The amount of energy required to remove the most loosely bound electron from an isolated gaseous atom is called ionisation energy.

The process may be represented as :

$A(g) + I.E. \rightarrow A^+ + e^-$ $I.E._1$ / $I.P_1$ $\Delta H = +ve$ (endothermic)

Ionisation energy is expressed either in terms of electron volts per atom (eV/atom) or kilo joules per mole of atoms (kJ/mol).

1 ev per atom = 96.3 kJ mol^{-1}

The ionisation energy defined above is more precisely the first ionisation energy (IE_1).

Successive Ionisation energies :

Once the first electron has been removed from the gaseous atom, it is possible to remove second electron from the monopositive ion.

The amount of energy required to remove the most loosely bound electron from the isolated monopositive ion of the element is called second ionisation energy (IE_2). Similarly, the energy required to remove the outermost electron from isolated dipositive ion is called third ionisation energy ($I.E._3$).

$A^+ (g) + I.E._1 \rightarrow A^+(g) + e^-$ $I.E._1$

$A^+ (g) + I.E._2 \rightarrow A^{2+}(g) + e^-$ $I.E._2$

$A^{2+} (g) + I.E._3 \rightarrow A^{3+}(g) + e^-$ $I.E._3$

The second (I.E.2), third (I.E.3), fourth (I.E.4) etc. ionisation energies are collectively known as successive ionisation energies. It may be noted that :

$\mathbf{IE_4 > IE_3 > IE_2 > IE_1}$

Factors on which Ionisation Energy Depends :

1. **Atomic Size :** I.E. decreases with increases in atomic size.
2. **Nuclear Charge :** I.E. increases with increase in nuclear charge.
3. **Screening Effect of the Inner Electrons :** Larger the number of electrons in the inner shells, greater is the screening effect on the outermost electron and hence lower is the ionisation energy.
4. **Penetration Effect :** Penetration power of various sub-shells of a particular energy level is in the order s > p > d > f. Therefore, for the same shell it is easier to remove an electron from p-sub-shell than from s-sub-shell. Greater the penetration power, higher is the I.E.
5. **Electronic Configuration :** The elements having stable electronic configurations have relatively higher values of I.E. For example,
   (i) The noble gases have stable configuration (ns^2np^6). They have highest ionisation energies within their respectively periods.

(ii) The elements like N($1s^2, 2s^2, 2p_x^1, 2p_y^1, 2p_z^1$) and P($1s^2, 2s^2, 2p^6, 3s^2, 3p_x^1, 3p_y^1, 3p_z^1$) have configurations in which orbitals belonging to same sub-shell are exactly half-filled. Such configurations are quite stable and consequently, their ionisation energies are relatively high.

(iii) The elements like Be ($1s^2, 2s^2$) and Mg ($1s^2, 2s^2, 2p^6, 3s^2$) have all electrons paired. Such configurations being stable also result in the higher values of ionisation energy.

Variation across the period : In general, the value of ionisation energy increases with the increases in atomic number across a period. This can be attributed to the fact that in moving across the period, nuclear charge increases and atomic size decreases regularly and hence, the electrons are more tightly bound to the nucleus.

This trend can be seen in ionization energies (in kJ mol^{-1}) of elements belonging to 2nd and 3rd periods.

2nd Period Elements

Element	Li	Be	B	C	N	O	F	Ne
Ionization Energy	520	899	801	1086	1400	1314	1680	2080

3rd Period Elements

Element	Na	Mg	Al	Si	P	S	Cl	Ar
Ionization Energy	496	738	578	786	1011	1000	1251	1521

Variation in a group : The value of ionisation energies decreases regularly with the increases in atomic number of shell and distance from the nucleus along a group.

We have already seen earlier, that the force of attraction between valence electrons and nucleus decrease in a group from top to bottom because of increase in atomic size due to addition of inner shells. Moreover, there is increase in shielding effect on outermost (valence) electrons due to increase in the number of inner electron. As a result,the electron becomes less and less firmly held to nucleus as we move down the group. Ionization energy decreases in a group from top to bottom. This can be seen from ioization energy values (in kJ mol^{-1}) of groups 1 and 17 elements given below :

Group 1		Group 17	
Element	**Ionization Energy**	**Element**	**Ionization Energy**
Li	520	F	1680
Na	496	Cl	1251
K	419	Br	1143
Rb	403	I	1009

$$\text{I.P.} \propto \frac{1}{\text{Atomic Size}}$$

I.P. $\propto$ Effective Nuclear Charge

$$\text{I.P.} \propto \frac{1}{\textit{Screening Effect}}$$

Note : Half filled and fully filled orbitals have greater ionisation potential.

Illustration 12

Out of Na^+ and Ne which has higher ionisation energy? Explain why.

Solution

Na^+ has higher ionisation energy than Ne. Na^+ and Ne are isoelectronic species. However, the nuclear charge in Na^+ is more than in Ne. Hence, the electrons are more tightly held in Na^+ and it has higher ionisation energy.

Illustration 13

Out of Al^+ and Mg^+ which has higher I.E.?

OR

Out of Al and Mg which has higher second I.E.?

Solution

In both Al^+ and Mg^+ the outermost electron is removed from 3s-orbital.

Al^+ : $1s^2, 2s^2, 2p^6, 3s^2$

Mg^+ : $1s^2, 2s^2, 2p^6, 2s^1$

Al^+ has higher I.E. than Mg^+ because nuclear charge in Al^+ (13 units) in higher than in Mg^+ (12 units). Moreover, Al^+ has stable configuration (Fully filled 2s sub-shell).

Illustration 14

(i) How do you think the tendency to lose electrons will change in a group?

(ii) How will this tendency change in a period ?

Solution

(i) Down the group, the effective nuclear charge experienced by valence electrons is decreasing because the outermost electrons are farther away from the nucleus. Therefore, the electrons can be easily lose.

(ii) As the effective nuclear charge acting on the valence shell electrons increases across a period, the tendency to lose electrons will decrease along the period.

(D) ELECTRON GAIN ENTHALPY / ELECTRON AFFINITY

Electron Gain Enthalpy may be defined as the amount of energy released when an electron is added to an isolated gaseous atom of the element.

The process may be expressed as :

$$A(g) + e^- \rightarrow A^-(g) + E.A. \qquad \Delta H = -ve \text{ (exothermic)}$$

The large value of electron reflects the greater tendency of an atom to accept the electron.

Units : The values of electron affinity are expressed either in electron volt per atom or kilo Joules per mole of atoms.

Factors Affecting Electron gain Enthalpy :

1. **Nuclear charge :** Greater the magnitude of nuclear charge, larger will be the value of electron affinity.
2. **Atomic size :** Larger the size of an atom, smaller will be the value of electron affinity.
3. **Electronic configuration. :** Stable the electronic configuration of an atom, lesser will be its tendency to accept the electron and lower will be the value of its electron affinity.

Variation in a period : On moving across the period the atomic size decreases and nuclear charge increases. Both these factors result into greater attraction for the incoming electron, therefore, **electron affinity, in general, increases in a period from left to right.** However, some irregularities are observed in general trends. These are mainly due to the stable electronic configurations of certain elements. For example, electron affinities of noble gases like nitrogen, beryllium and magnesium are negative (regarded as zero) due to their stable electronic configurations.

Variation along a group : On moving down a group, the atomic size and nuclear charge increase but the effect of increase in atomic size is much more pronounced that of nuclear charge and thus the additional electron feels less attraction by the nucleus.

Such trends in its values (in kJ mol^{-1}) for group 1 and group 17 elements are given below.

Group 1		Group 17	
Element	**Electron Affinity**	**Element**	**Electron Affinity**
Li	58	F	333
Na	53	Cl	348
K	48	Br	324
Rb	45	I	295

Consequently, electron affinity decreases from top to bottom in a group. However, electron affinities of elements of the second period are lower than those for the elements of the third period. This is possibly due to the strong inter electron repulsion forces operating within the relatively compact 2p-sub-shell.

Illustration 15

(i) ***How would the tendency to gain electrons change as you go from left to right across a period?***

(ii) ***How would the tendency to gain electrons change as you go down a group?***

Solution

As the trends in the electronegativity show, non-metals are found on the right hand side of the Periodic Table towards the top.
These trends also help us to predict the nature of oxides formed by the elements because it is known that the oxides of metals are basic and that of non-metals are acidic in general.

Illustration 16

Arrange F, Cl, Br and I in the decreasing order of their electron gain enthalpies and give an account for the order assigned.

Solution

The decreasing order of electon affinities is Cl > F > Br > I.
In case of fluorine electron goes to second energy level which is very small in size and has already seven electrons present in it. Therefore, the added electron feels some repulsion from the electrons already present in the valence shell. This neutralises to some extent the attractive force of nucleus on the electron being added.
On the other hand in chlorine added electron goes to third energy level which is of larger size. Hence electron affinity of fluorine is less than that of chlorine.

$F + e^- \rightarrow F^-$

$1s^2, 2s^2, 2p^5$

$Cl + e^- \rightarrow Cl^-$

On the other hand, if we compare the electron affinities of Cl and Br, then electron affinity of Cl is more than that of Br because Cl atom is smaller in size and hence effective nuclear charge in Cl is more than in Br. Therefore, added electron is more strongly attracted in Cl. Similarly, electron affinity of Br is higher than that of I. So, the overall of electron affinities of halogens is Cl > Br > I.

$$E.A. = \frac{1}{\text{Atomic Size}}$$

$$EA \propto Z_{eff.}$$

Illustration 17

In each of the following sets arrange the elements in the increasing order of their electron affinities:

(i) C, N, O (ii) O, N, S (iii) S, Cl, Ar (iv) F, Cl, Br

Solution

(i) N < C < O (ii) N < O < S (iii) Ar < S < Cl (iv) Br < F < Cl

(E) ELECTRONEGATIVITY

Electronegativity may be defined as the tendency of an atom in a molecule to attract towards itself the shared pair of electrons.

The main factors on which the electronegativity depends are effective nuclear charge and atomic radius.

$$\text{Electronegativity} \propto \text{Effective Nuclear Charge}$$

$$\text{Electronegativity} \propto \frac{1}{\text{size}}$$

Electronegativity have no unit.

In period : electronegativity increases in moving from left to right. This is due to the reason that nuclear charge increases whereas atomic radius decreases as we move from left to right in a period. Halogens have the highest value of electronegativity in their respective periods.

2nd Period Elements

Element	Li	Be	B	C	N	O	F
Electronegativity	1.0	1.5	2.0	2.5	3.0	3.5	4.0

3rd Period Elements

Element	Na	Mg	Al	Si	P	S	Cl
Electronegativity	0.9	1.2	1.5	1.8	2.1	2.5	3.0

In a group : electronegativity decreases on moving down the group. This is due to the effect of increased atomic radius.

Group 1		**Group 17**	
Element	**Electronegativity**	**Element**	**Electronegativity**
Li	1.0	**F**	**4.0**
Na	0.9	Cl	3.0
K	0.8	Br	2.8
Rb	0.8	I	2.5

$$E.N. \propto \frac{1}{\text{Atomic Size}}$$

E.N. $\propto$ % s-character hybridise atom

E.N. $\propto$ Oxidation State

$Mn^{+2} < Mn^{+4} < Mn^{+7}$

1. ***Fluorine atom has the greatest power of attracting electrons and is the most electronegative element.***
2. ***Halogens have the highest electronegativities.***
3. ***Non-metals have high electronegativity values in comparison to metals.***
4. ***(N, Cl = 3.0), (C, S, I = 2.5), (Be, Al = 1.5), (P, H = 2.1), (Cs, Fr = 0.7)***

5.11 SOME IMPORTANT NOTES :

Based on number of incomplete shells the elements are classified into four types. Inert gases, representative elements, transition elements and inner transition elements.

(a) General electronic configuration of inert gases (except He) is ns^2np^6 (outermost shell completely filled.)

(b) In representative elements,only the outermost shell is incomplete. General electronic configurations varies from ns^1 to $ns^2\ np^6$.

(c) In transition elements, two outer most shells are incomplete (nth and (n – 1)th). General electronic configuration is $(n-1)\,d^{1-10}\,ns^{1-2}$.

(d) In inner transition elements, three outer shells are incomplete. General electronic configuration is $(n-2)f^{1-14}\,(n-1)d^{0-1}\,ns^2$.

Diagonal Relationship :- Certain elements of second period exhibit similarty in properties as shown by the elements diagonally placed to them in the third row, e.g. This is called **diagonal relationship.** Li and Mg; Be and Al; B and Si shows diagonal relationship.

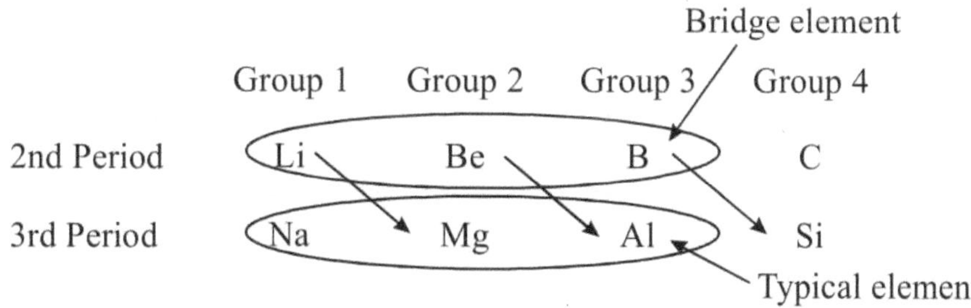

This is due to identical ionic radii and polarizing power (i.e., charge/ size ratio of the pairs of these elements). Elements of second period are known as **bridge elements.**

Anomalous behaviour of first element of a group.

The first element of a group exhibits difference in its properties in certain respects from the rest of the elements of its group. This is due to its small size, high electronegativity and non avaiability of d-electrons. This anomalous behaviour is shown by the elements of the second row (period) i.e. , Li to F.

Typical Element : These elements represent the properties of other element of respective group.

Some Important General Periodic Trends

	PERIODS	GROUPS
IONISATION ENTHALPY	INCREASES →	DECREASES ↓
ELECTRON AFFINITY	INCREASES →	DECREASES ↓
ATOMIC RADII	DECREASES →	INCREASES ↓
ELECTRONEGATIVITY	INCREASES →	DECREASES ↓

SOLVED EXAMPLES

Example 1

Explain why there are only 18 elements in the fifth period.

Solution

The fifth period begins with the filling of 5s orbital and continious fill the filling of sixth energy level (6s) starts. The sub-shells which follow 5s are, 4d, 5p, 6s .... Thus, the elements which involve filling of 5s, 4d and 5p, subshells can accept 18 electrons in all, there are 18 elements in the fifth period.

Example 2

Out of Al and Al^{3+} which has smaller size and why?

Solution

Al^{3+} is formed by removal of 3 electrons from Al. Thus number of electrons in Al^{3+}, is three less than the number of electrons in Al whereas both have same nuclear charge. Therefore, electrons are more tightly held in Al^{3+}, the outer-most shell is second. Hence, Al^{3+} is smaller in size than Al.

$_{13}Al$: $1s^2, 2s^2, 2p^6, 3s^2, 3p_x^{\ 1}$.

Example 3

Arrange Mg, Mg^+ and Mg^{2+} in the increasing order of their sizes. Give explanation for the order assigned.

Solution

Mg, Mg^+ and Mg^{2+} have same nuclear charge (12 units) however, the number of electrons in them is 12, 11 and 10 respectively. Therefore, Mg^{2+}, having least number of electrons, is the smallest whereas Mg, having maximum number of electrons, is the largest. The increasing order of their size is :

$Mg^{2+} < Mg^+ < Mg$

Example 4

How do you explain that $_{31}Ga$ has slightly higher I.E. than $_{13}Al$, although it occupies lower position in the group?

Solution

$_{13}Al$: $1s^2, 2s^2, 2p^6, 3s^2, 3p^1$

$_{13}Ga$: $1s^2, 2s^2, 2p^6, 3s^2, 3p^6, 3d^{10}, 4s^2, 4p^1$

In Ga, the 10 electrons present in 3d-sub-shell do not shield the outer electrons from the nucleus effectively. As a result effective nuclear charge in Ga increases. This explains why I.E. of Ga is slightly more than that of $_{13}Al$.

Example 5

Out of Ca^{2+}, and Ar which has higher ionisation energy ? Explain briefly.

Solution

Ca^{2+} and Ar are isoelectronic and have 18 electrons each. However, nuclear charge of Ca^{2+}, is 20 whereas that of Ar is 18. Due to higher nuclear charge. electrons in Ca^{2+} are more tightly held and hence it has higher ionisation energy than Ar.

Example 6

Out of aluminium and magnesium which has higher ionisation energy and why?

Solution

Aluminium and magesium belong to same period. Nuclear charge in Al is 13 and in Mg it is 12. So, it is expected that Al should have higher I.E. than Mg. But if we carefully observe the electronic configurations of Al and Mg then we find that Mg has stable configuration (Fully filled s-Sub-shell in valence shell) and hence has higher ionization energy than Al. Moreover in Mg, the electron is removed from 3s-orbital which, due to high penetration and less shielding by the electrons in the lower orbitals, experiences stronger force attraction from nucleus as compared with 3p electron of Al. Therefore, Mg has higher ionisation energy than Al.

$_{13}Al$: $1s^2, 2s^2, 2p^6, 3s^2, 3p_x^{\ 1}$

$_{12}Mg$: $1s^2, 2s^2, 2p^6, 3s^2$

Example 7

Out of Al^+ and Mg^+ which, has higher I.E.?

or

Out of Al and Mg which has higher second I.E.?

Solution

Al^+ has higher second I.E. because nuclear charge in Al^+ (13 units) is higher than in Mg^+ (12 units) and Al^+ has stable configuration (Fully filled 3s sub-shell).

Example 8

Arrange F, Cl, Br and I in the decreasing order of their electron affinities and account for the order assigned.

Solution

The decreasing order of electron affinities is Cl > F > Br > I.

In case of fluorine added electron goes to second energy electron feels some repulsion from the electrons already present in the valence shell. On the other hand, in chlorine added electron goes to third level which is of larger size. Hence, **electron affinity of fluorine is less than that of chlorine.**

$F + e^- \rightarrow F^-$

$Cl + e^- \rightarrow Cl^-$

on the other hand, if we compare the electron affinities of Cl and Br then electron affinity of Cl is more than that of Br because Cl atom is smaller in size and hence effective nuclear charge in Cl is more than in Br. Therefore, added electron is more strongly attracted in Cl. Similarly, electron affinity of Br is higher than that of I. So, the overall order of electron affinities of halogens is Cl > F > Br > I.

Example 9

Explain why electron affinities of noble gases are zero.

Solution

All noble gases have ns^2np^6 valence shell configuration (except helium where it is $1s^2$). In the valence shell of noble gases s and p sub-shells are fully filled, therefore, these configurations are highly stable. Hence, noble gases do not have any tendency to accept more electrons because this would disturb their stable configuration. Hence, electron affinities of noble gases are zero.

Example 10

Given on the side is a part of the periodic table. As we move vertically downward from Li to Fr

(a) What happens to the size of the atom from Li to Fr.

(b) What happens to their metallic character?

Solution

(a) When we move vertically downward from Li to Fr the atomic size increases, i.e. Fr is the biggest atom.

(b) The metallic character increases i.e Fr is the most metallic element (Tendency of large electrons)

Example 11

Given below is a part of the periodic table

Li	Be	B	*l*	N	O	F
Na	Mg	Al	Si	P	S	Cl

As we move horizontally from left to right

(a) What happens to the metallic character of the elements?

(b) What happens to the atomic size?

Solution

(a) When we move horizontally from left to right, the metallic character decreases.

(b) When we move horizontally from left to right, the atomic size decreases.

Example 12

Element (X) forms a chloride with the formula XCl_2, Which is a solid with high melting point. (X) would most likely be in the same group of the periodic table as

(a) Na (b) Mg (c) Al (d) Si (e) P

Solution

The element (X) should have last two electrons to form XCl_2. So (X) belongs to group 2. Therefore, the element (X) lies in the same group as magnesium (Mg). So the answer (b) is correct.

Example 13

How do the electronic structures of the atoms relate to their position in the modern periodic table?

Solution

In the modern periodic table, the period describes the number of electronic shells in the atom and the last entering electrons in the outer most sub-shell denote the group. So the location of any element in the periodic table is related to their position/location in the periodic table.

CONCEPT APPLICATION LEVEL - I [NCERT Questions]

Q.1 Did Dobereiner's triads also exist in the columns of Newlands' Octaves? Compare and find out.

Ans. Only one triad of Dobereiner's triads exists in the columns of Newlands' octaves. The triad formed by the elements Li, Na, and K of Dobereiner's triads also occurred in the columns of Newlands' octaves.
Dobereiner's triads

Li	Ca	Cl
Na	Sr	Br
K	Ba	I

Newlands' octaves

H	Li	Be	B	C	N	O
F	Na	Mg	Al	Si	P	S
Cl	K	Ca	Cr	Ti	Mn	Fe
Co and Ni	Cu	Zn	Y	In	As	Se
Br	Rb	Sr	Ce and La	Zr	–	–

Q.2 What were the limitations of Dobereiner's classification?

Ans. Limitation of Dobereiner's classification:
All known elements could not be classified into groups of triads on the basis of their properties.

Q.3 What were the limitations of Newlands' Law of Octaves?

Ans. Limitations of Newlands' law of octaves:

(i) It was not applicable throughout the arrangements. It was applicable up to calcium only. The properties of the elements listed after calcium showed no resemblance to the properties of the elements above them.

(ii) Those elements that were discovered after Newlands' octaves did not follow the law of octaves.

(iii) The position of cobalt and nickel in the group of the elements (F, Cl) of different properties could not be explained.

(iv) Placing of iron far away from cobalt and nickel, which have similar properties as iron, could also not be explained.

Q.4 Use Mendeleev's Periodic Table to predict the formulae for the oxides of the following elements: K, C, Al, Si, Ba.

Ans. K is in group 1. Therefore, the oxide will be K_2O.
C is in group 4. Therefore, the oxide will be CO_2.
Al is in group 3. Therefore, the oxide will be Al_2O_3.
Si is in group 4. Therefore, the oxide will be SiO_2.
Ba is in group 2. Therefore, the oxide will be BaO.

Q.5 Besides gallium, which other elements have since been discovered that were left by Mendeleev in his Periodic Table? (any two)

Ans. Scandium and germanium

Q.6 What were the criteria used by Mendeleev in creating his Periodic Table?

Ans. Mendeleev's periodic table was based on the observation that the properties of elements are a periodic function of their atomic masses. This means that if elements are arranged in the increasing order of their atomic masses, then their properties get repeated after regular intervals.

Q.7 Why do you think the noble gases are placed in a separate group?

Ans. Noble gases are inert elements. Their properties are different from the all other elements. Therefore, the noble gases are placed in a separate group.

Q.8 How could the Modern Periodic Table remove various anomalies of Mendeleev's Periodic Table?

Ans. Mendeleev was unable to give fixed position to hydrogen and isotopes in the periodic table. In Mendeleev's periodic table, the increasing manner of atomic mass of the elements is not always regular from one to its next. It was believed that a more fundamental property than atomic mass could explain periodic properties in a better manner.

It was Henry Moseley who demonstrated that atomic number of an element could explain periodic properties in a better way than atomic mass of an element and arranged the elements in increasing order of their atomic numbers. Then it was found that the various anomalies of Mendeleev's periodic table were removed by the modern periodic table.

Q.9 Name two elements you would expect to show chemical reactions similar to magnesium. What is the basis for your choice?

Ans. Calcium (Ca) and strontium (Sr) are expected to show chemical reactions similar to magnesium (Mg). This is because the number of valence electrons (2) is same in all these three elements. And since chemical properties are due to valence electrons, they show same chemical reactions.

Q.10 Name

(a) three elements that have a single electron in their outermost shells.

(b) two elements that have two electrons in their outermost shells.

(c) three elements with filled outermost shells.

Ans. (a) Lithium (Li), sodium (Na), and potassium (K) have a single electron in their outermost shells.

(b) Magnesium (Mg) and calcium (Ca) have two electrons in their outermost shells.

(c) Neon (Ne), argon (Ar), and xenon (Xe) have filled outermost shells.

Q.11 (a) Lithium, sodium, potassium are all metals that react with water to liberate hydrogen gas. Is there any similarity in the atoms of these elements?

(b) Helium is an unreactive gas and neon is a gas of extremely low reactivity. What do their atoms have in common?

Ans. (a) Yes. The atoms of all the three elements lithium, sodium, and potassium have one electron in their outermost shells.

(b) Both helium (He) and neon (Ne) have filled outermost shells. Helium has a duplet in its K shell, while neon has an octet in its L shell.

Q.12 In the Modern Periodic Table, which are the metals among the first ten elements?

Ans. Among the first ten elements, lithium (Li) and beryllium (Be) are metals.

Q.13 By considering their position in the Periodic Table, which one of the following elements would you expect to have maximum metallic characteristic?
Ga, Ge, As, Se, Be

Ans. Since Be lies to the extreme left hand side of the periodic table, Be is the most metallic among the given elements.

Q.14 Which of the following statements is not a correct statement about the trends when going from left to right across the periods of periodic Table.
(a) The elements become less metallic in nature.
(b) The number of valence electrons increases.
(c) The atoms lose their electrons more easily.
(d) The oxides become more acidic.

Ans. (c) The atoms lose their electrons more easily.
(On moving from left to right across the periods of the periodic table, ionisation potential increases. Hence, the tendency to lose electrons decreases.)

Q.15 Element X forms a chloride with the formula XCl_2, which is a solid with a high melting point. X would most likely be in the same group of the Periodic Table as
(a) Na (b) Mg (c) Al (d) Si

Ans. (b) X would most likely be in the same group of the Periodic Table as magnesium (Mg).

Q.16 Which element has
(a) two shells, both of which are completely filled with electrons?
(b) the electronic configuration 2, 8, 2?
(c) a total of three shells, with four electrons in its valence shell?
(d) a total of two shells, with three electrons in its valence shell?
(e) twice as many electrons in its second shell as in its first shell?

Ans. (a) Neon has two shells, both of which are completely filled with electrons (2 electrons in K shell and 8 electrons in L shell).
(b) Magnesium has the electronic configuration 2, 8, 2.
(c) Silicon has a total of three shells, with four electrons in its valence shell (2 electrons in K shell, 8 electrons in L shell and 4 electrons in M shell).
(d) Boron has a total of two shells, with three electrons in its valence shell (2 electrons in K shell and 3 electrons in L shell).
(e) Carbon has twice as many electrons in its second shell as in its first shell (2 electrons in K shell and 4 electrons in L shell).

Q.17 (a) What property do all elements in the same column of the Periodic Table as boron have in common?
(b) What property do all elements in the same column of the Periodic Table as fluorine have in common?

Ans. (a) All the elements in the same column as boron have the same number of valence electrons (3). Hence, they all have valency equal to 3.
(b) All the elements in the same column as fluorine have the same number of valence electrons (7). Hence, they all have valency equal to 1.

Q.18 An atom has electronic configuration 2, 8, 7.

(a) What is the atomic number of this element?

(b) To which of the following elements would it be chemically similar? (Atomic numbers are given in parentheses.)

N(7) F(9) P(15) Ar(18)

Ans. (a) The atomic number of this element is 17.

(b) It would be chemically similar to F(9) with configuration as 2, 7.

Q.19 The position of three elements A, B and C in the Periodic Table are shown below ?

Group 16	Group 17
–	–
–	A
–	–
B	C

(a) State whether A is a metal or non-metal.

(b) State whether C is more reactive or less reactive than A.

(c) Will C be larger or smaller in size than B?

(d) Which type of ion, cation or anion, will be formed by element A?

Ans. (a) A is a non-metal.

(b) C is less reactive than A, as reactivity decreases down the group in halogens.

(c) C will be smaller in size than B as moving across a period, the nuclear charge increases and therefore, electrons come closer to the nucleus.

(d) A will form an anion as it accepts an electron to complete its octet.

Q.20 Nitrogen (atomic number 7) and phosphorus (atomic number 15) belong to group 15 of the Periodic Table. Write the electronic configuration of these two elements. Which of these will be more electronegative? Why?

Ans.

Element	K	L	M
Nitrogen	2	5	
Phosphorus	2	8	5

Nitrogen is more electronegative than phosphorus. On moving down a group, the number of shell increases. Therefore, the valence electrons move away from the nucleus and the effective nuclear charge decreases. This causes the decrease in the tendency to attract electron and hence electronegativity decreases.

Q.21 How does the electronic configuration of an atom relate to its position in the Modern Periodic Table?

Ans. In the modern periodic table, atoms with similar electronic configurations are placed in the same column. In a group, the number of valence electrons remain the same. Elements across a period show an increase in the number of valence electrons.

Q.22 In the Modern Periodic Table, calcium (atomic number 20) is surrounded by elements with atomic numbers 12, 19, 21 and 38. Which of these have physical and chemical properties resembling calcium?

Ans. The element with atomic number 12 has same chemical properties as that of calcium. This is because both of them have same number of valence electrons (2).

Q.23 Compare and contrast the arrangement of elements in Mendeleev's periodic Table and the Modern Periodic Table.

Ans.

S.No.	Mendeleev's Periodic Table	S.No.	Modern Periodic Table
1	Elements are arranged in the increasing order of their atomic masses.	1	Elements are arranged in the increasing order of their atomic numbers.
2	There are a total of 7 groups (columns) and 6 periods (rows).	2	There are a total of 18 groups (columns) and 7 periods (rows).
3	Elements having similar properties were placed directly under one another.	3	Elements having the same valence shell are present in the same period while elements having the same number of valence electrons are present in the same group.
4	The position of hydrogen could not be explained.	4	Hydrogen is placed above alkali metals.
5	No distinguishing positions for metals and non-metals.	5	Metals are present at the left hand side of the periodic table whereas non-metals are present at the right hand side.

CONCEPT APPLICATION LEVEL - II [Previous Year Questions]

SECTION - A

MULTIPLE CHOICE QUESTIONS (ONE CORRECT ANSWER) :

Q.1 Which of the following statements is not a correct statement about the trends when going from left to right across the periods of the periodic table ?
(A) The element become less metallic in nature
(B) The number of valence electron increases
(C) The atoms lose their electrons more easily
(D) The oxides become more acidic

Q.2 The electronic configuration of the atom of an element X is 2, 8, 4. In modern periodic table, the element X is placed in :
(A) 2nd group (B) 4th group (C) 14th group (D) 8th group

Q.3 Which of the following element does not lose an electron easily ?
(A) Na (B) F (C) Mg (D) Al

Q.4 An element which is an essential constituent of all organic compounds belongs to following group of modern periodic table
(A) group 4 (B) group 14 (C) group 15 (D) group 16

Q.5 On moving from left to right in a period of the periodic table, the atomic number of elements increases. What happens to the size of atoms of element on moving from left to right in a period?
(A) increases (B) decreases
(C) remains the same (D) first increases then decreases

Q.6 Which of the following set of elements is written correctly in the order of their increasing metallic character?
(A) Mg, Al, Si (B) C, O, N (C) Na, Li, K (D) Be, Mg, Ca

Q.7 In Mendeleev's periodic table, gap was not left for one of the following elements. This element is:
(A) gallium (B) beryllium (C) germanium (D) scandium

Q.8 The Newland's law of octaves for the classification of elements was found to be applicable only up to the element
(A) potassium (B) calcium (C) cobalt (D) phosphorus

Q.9 The three elements having chemical symbols of Si, B and Ge are
(A) all metals (B) all non-metals
(C) all metalloids (D) Si is metalloid, B is metal and Ge is non-metal

Q.10 An element X forms an oxide X_2O_3. In which group of Mendeev's periodic table is this element placed?
(A) group I (B) group II (C) group V (D) group VIII

SECTION -B

VERY SHORT ANSWSER TYPE QUESTIONS [1 Mark]

Q.1 Lithium, sodium and potassium form a Dobereiner's triad. The atomic mass of lithium and potassium are 7 and 39 respectively. Predict the atomic mass of sodium.

Ans. Atomic mass of sodium will be the average of atomic mass of lithium and potassium, i.e., Atomic mass of sodium $= \frac{7+39}{2} = \frac{46}{2} = 23$. It is very near to the actual atomic mass of sodium which is 22.9894.

Q.2 Calcium, Strontium and Barium form a Dobereiner's triad. The atomic masses of Calcium and Barium are 40 and 137 respectively. Predict the atomic mass of strontium.

Ans. Atomic mass of Strontium will be the average of atomic mass of Calcium and Barium, i.e.,

$$\text{Atomic mass of Strontium} = \frac{\text{Atomic mass of Calcium + Atomic mass of Barium.}}{2}$$

$$= \frac{40+137}{2} = 88.5$$

Q.3 Is it possible to have an element with atomic number 1.5 placed between hydrogen and helium?

Ans. No, it is not possible because the atomic numbers of elements are always in whole numbers.

Q.4 A metal M forms an oxide having the formula M_2O_3. It belongs to 3rd period in the Modern Periodic table . Write the atomic number and valency of the metal.

Ans. Atomic number of the element (metal) is 13 and valency of the metal is three.

Q.5 State modern periodic law of classification of elements.

Ans. Properties of elements are periodic functions of their atomic numbers.

Q.6 State modern periodic law on which side of the periodic table do you find (i) metals (ii) non-metal?

Ans. Modern periodic law : "The properties of elements are the periodic function of their atomic number". Metals are placed on the left side while non-metals are placed on the right side of the periodic table.

Q.7 How many triads were identified by Dobereiner ? Name any one of them. **[CBSE-2012]**

Ans. Three triads were identified by Dobereiner. One such triad was of lithium, sodium and potassium.

Q.8 Give any one characteristic of Dobereiner triads. **[CBSE-2010]**

Ans. Atomic mass of the middle element was roughly the average of the atomic masses of other two elements.

Q.9 Give any one limitation of Dobereiner classification. **[CBSE-2011]**

Ans. He could identify only three triads from the elements known at that time.

Q.10 Name any two pair of elements which were adjusted by Newland in the same slot. **[CBSE-2011]**

Ans. (i) Cobalt and nickel (ii) Cerium and lanthanum

Q.11 Define Newland's law of Octaves.

Ans. The properties of every eighth element is similar to that of the first element

Q.12 Name any two elements which were discovered later after. Mendeleev's periodic table. **[CBSE-2011]**
Ans. Gallium and germanium.

Q.13 The electronic configuration of an element is 2, 8, 7. Identify whether it is a metal or non-metal? Also, name the element. **[CBSE-2012]**
Ans. It is a non-metal. It is chlorine.

Q.14 Atomic radius of hydrogen is 37 pm. Express it in metre. **[CBSE-2012]**
Ans. 3.7×10^{-11} m (1 pm = 10^{-12} m).

Q.15 How atomic size vary in a group and in a period? **[CBSE-2012]**
Ans. Atomic size increases in a group and decreases in a period.

Q.16 In which part of the periodic table we can look for metalloids. On which side of these we can get non-metals ? **[CBSE-2012]**
Ans. (a) Metalloids are present in between metals and non-metals on the right hand side of the periodic table.
(b) Non-metals are present on the right hand side.

Q.17 What is the significance of knowing position of element in the periodic table ? **[CBSE-2012]**
Ans. The position of an element in the periodic table tells us about its chemical reactivity.

SHORT ANSWSER TYPE QUESTIONS [2 Marks]

Q.1 Atomic number is considered to be a more appropriate parameter than atomic mass for classification of elements in a periodic table. Why ?
How does metallic character of elements vary on moving from :
(i) left to right in a period
(ii) from top to bottom in a group

Ans. The properties of the elements could be predicted more precisely when elements are arranged on the basis of increasing atomic number. The atomic number is equal to the number of protons and which are equal to the number of electrons. It is the number of electrons which decide the properties of the element.
(i) **Decreases :** This is due to an increase in nuclear charge which tends to pull the electrons closer to the nucleus and reduce the size of the atom
(ii) **Increases :** This is because new shells are being added as we go down the group. It increases the distance between the nucleus and the valence shell.

Q.2 Study the variation in the atomic radii of first group elements given below and arrange tem in a increasing order.
(i) Name the elements which have the smallest and the largest atoms

Group I elements	Na	Li	Rb	Cs	K
Atomic radius (pm)	861	152	244	262	231

(ii) How does the atomic size vary as you go down a group ?

Ans. (i) The element having the smallest atom is lithium (Atomic radius is 152 pm) while the element having the largest atom is cesium (Atomic radius is 262 pm)
(ii) The atomic size increases while going down a group because new shells are being added at each step

Q.3 State the positions of (i) isotopes of the same element and (ii) hydrogen in the modern periodic table. **[CBSE-2012]**

Ans. (i) Position of isotopes in the same slot
(ii) Hydrogen in the first group and first period.

Q.4 How does (a) metallic character and (a) atomic size vary :
(i) in a group (ii) a period ? **[CBSE-2012]**

Ans. **(a) Metallic character :** **In a group :** Increases from top to bottom
In a period : Decreases from left to right
(b) Atomic size : **In a group :** Increases from top to bottom
In a period : Decreases from left to right.

Q.5 Arrange the following elements in the descending order of atomic size and give a reason for your answer.
Mg, Cl, P, Ar (Atomic number of elements are : 12, 17, 15, 18) **[CBSE-2012]**

Ans. Descending order of atomic size :

Mg	P	Cl	Ar

Reason : They all belong to the same period and in a period, atomic size decreases due to the increases in the nuclear charge.

Q.6 "Elements in periodic table show periodicity of properties." List any four such properties. **[CBSE-2012, 2013]**

Ans. (i) Atomic size (ii) Valency or combining capacity
(iii) Metallic character (iv) Non-metallic character

Q.7 State modern periodic law. What are vertical columns and horizontal rows in a periodic table known as ? **[Delhi-2013]**

Ans. Moder periodic law : "Properties of elements are a periodic function of their atomic number."
In modern periodic table, there are :
(i) 18 vertical columns called GROUPS. (ii) 7 horizontal rows called PERIODS.

Q.8 Na, Mg, Al and P belong to 3rd period but are placed in first, second, thirteenth and fifteenth group. Number of shells occupied in Mg is three. What is the number of occupied shells in Na, Al and P. Give reason for your answer. **[CBSE-2013]**

Ans. It is three in Na, Al and P. Elements with the same number of occupied shells are placed in same period.

Q.9 The elements of third period are given below :
Na, Mg, Al, Si, P, S, Cl
(a) which is more metallic, S or Cl and why ?
(b) which has higher atomic mass, Al or C ?
(c) which is more electronegative, S or Cl and why ?

Ans. (a) Metallic character (electropositive character) decreases on moving from left to right in a period. This is because as the nuclear charge increases in a period, it becomes more difficult for the atoms to lose electrons, i.e., they become less electropositive. Hence, sulphur is more metallic than chlorine.
(b) Chlorine has higher atomic mass than that of aluminium
(c) Electronegative character (non-metallic character) increases with increase in atomic number in a period. Due to increased nuclear charge in a period, it becomes easier for the atoms to gain electrons and they become more electronegative. Hence, chlorine is more electronegative than sulphur.

LONGANSWSER TYPE QUESTIONS [3 Marks]

Q.1 (a) What is meant by periodicity in properties of elements with reference to the periodic table ?
(b) Why do all the elements of the same group have similar properties?
(c) How will the tendency to gain electrons change as we go from left to right across a period? Why ? **[Delhi-2013]**

Ans. (a) Recurrence of similar properties of elements after certain fixed interval of atomic number.
(b) They have similar properties because.
(i) They all have same number of valence electrons.
(ii) They all have same valency.
(c) The tendency to gain electrons increases due to increase in the nuclear charge. Due to this, atomic size decreases and a large number of valence electrons are held towards the nucleus and tendency to gain electrons increases.

Q.2 What physical and chemical properties of elements were used by Mendeleev in creating his periodic table? List two observations which posed a challenge to Mendeleev's Periodic Law. **[Delhi-2013]**

Ans. Among physical properties, elements were arranged on the basis of their atomic mass.
Among chemical properties, Mendeleev, Concentrated on the compounds formed by element with oxygen and hydrogen.
Two observation which posed a challenge to Mendeleev's periodic Law:
(i) Isotopes of all elements, as they could not be accommodated in the periodic table
(ii) Atomic massess do not increase in a regular manner in going from one element to the next.

Q.3 The position of four element A, B, C and D is the periodic table are shown below :

Group–I	**Group-17**
....	
....	................B...............
...............D.............	....
....	....
....	....
.................A.............	..................C.............

(a) Name most electronegative element.
(b) Name most reactive metal.
(c) State whether B is a metal or a non-metal
(d) Which one of the given element is expected to have largest atomic radius ?
(e) How many electrons are present in the outermost shell of elements B and C ?
(f) What will be the nature of the bond formed between D and B ?

Ans. (a) Most electronegative element -B
(b) Most reactive metal - A
(c) B is a non - metal
(d) A has largest atomic radius
(e) No. of valence electron in B and C - 7 electrons
(f) Nature of bond between D and B - ionic / electrovalent.

Q.4 From the part of a periodic table, answer the following questions :

1 Lithium	2	13	14 Carbon	15	16 Oxygen	17 Fluorine
X			P			Q
Y						R
Z						T

(a) Which is the most reactive metal ?

(b) Name the family of fluorine Q, R, T

(c) Name one element each of group 2 and 15

(d) Give the name of the element P placed below carbon

(e) Compare X and P with respect to size of atoms **[CBSE-2012]**

Ans. (a) Z (Reactivity increases downwards in a metallic group)

(b) Halogen

(c) Group 2 : Beryllium, magnesium.
Group 15 : Nitrogen, phosphorus.

(d) Silicon

(e) Size of X is bigger than P because atomic size decreases in a period.

Q.5 (a) How does the tendency to gain electrons change as we go down a group ? Give reason.

(b) Given below is a part of the periodic table. How does the valency vary, as we move vertically downward from Li to Fr ? Given reason **[CBSE-2012]**

Li	Be
Na	
K	
Rb	
Cs	
Fr	Ra

Ans. (a) Tendency to gain electrons decreases down a group because of decrease in the nuclear charge

(b) Valency remains same in the group because in a group valence electrons remain the same.

Q.6 What are metalloids ? Name four metalloids. **[CBSE-2012, Delhi-2013]**

Ans. The borderline elements present between metals and non-metals having properties in-between metals and non-metals are called metalloids or semi-metals.

Examples :

(i) Boron (B) (ii) Silicon (Si) (iii) Germanium (Ge)

(iv) Arsenic (As) (v) Antimony (Sb) (vi) Tellurium (Te)

(vii) Polonium (Po) (any four)

Q.7 An element A on combining with oxygen produces an oxide A_2O which is basic in nature. Now answer the following questions :

(i) How many electrons must be there in the outermost shell of the element A?

(ii) To which group of periodic table it belongs?

(iii) Identify whether it is a metal or a non-metal?

Ans. (i) A forms A_2O, means 2 electrons are given to oxygen atom by 2 atoms of A. So each A atom has 1 electron in its outermost shell.

(ii) A belongs to I-group of periodic table.

(iii) A is a metal.

Q.8 (a) What property do all elements in the same column of the periodic table as boron have in common?

(b) What property do all elements in the same column of the periodic table as fluorine have in common?

Ans. (a) All the elements of 12th group in which boron in present have 3 electrons in their valence shell.

(b) Fluorine belongs to 17th group. All elements of this group have 7 electrons in their valence shell

VERY LONG ANSWSER TYPE QUESTIONS [5 Marks]

Q.1 (a) Which two criteria did Mendeleev use to classify the elements in his periodic table ?

(b) State Mendeleev's periodic law.

(c) Why could no fixed position be given to hydrogen in Mendeleev's periodic table ?

(d) How and why does the atomic size vary as you go :

(i) from left to right along a period ?

(ii) down a group ?

Or

(a) Why did Mendeleev have gaps in his periodic table ?

(b) State any three limitations of Mendeleev's classification .

(c) How do electronic configurations of atoms change in a period with increase in atomic number?

Ans. (a) Two criteria used by Mendeleev to classify the elements in his periodic table were:

(i) Atomic mass.

(ii) Chemical properties, i.e., reaction with oxygen and hydrogen.

(b) Mendeleev's periodic law states that 'properties of the elements are periodic functions of their atomic masses.'

(c) No fixed position could be given to hydrogen in Mendeleev's periodic table because it resembles its properties both with alkali metals i.e., Li, Na, k, etc. and Halogens i.e., F, Cl, Br, etc.

(d) (i) From left to right along a period, atomic size decreases with the increase in electrons in the same shell hence the increase in effective nuclear charge.

(ii) Down a group, atomic size increase in with the increase in number of shells getting precedence over the nulcear charge.

Or

(a) Mendeleev had gaps in his periodic table for the element to be discovered in future. Mendeleev didn't see them as defects but boldly predicted their presence.

(b) Three limitations of Mendeleev's classification are :

(i) **Anamolous pairs :** Mendeleev's couldn't explain the presence of anamolous pairs in which an element with more atomic mass preceed the element with lower atomic mass, e.g., Co and Ni.

(ii) **Position of Isotopes :** Though, Mendeleev's periodic table was based upon atomic mass yet, no separate position were there for different isotopes of element (having different masses but same atomic number).

(iii) **Position of Hydrogen :** There was no fixed position of hydrogen since its properties resemble both with Group I elements and Group VII elements.

(c) With the increase in atomic number in a period, an electron is added successively increasing from 1 to 8 to the outermost (valence) shell. While in a period, the number of shells remain the same.

Q.2 The atomic radii of the element of second period are given below :

Second period elements	B	Be	O	N	Li	F	C
Atomic Radii (pm)	88	111	66	74	152	64	77

(i) Arrange these elements in decreasing order of their atomic radii.

(ii) Are the elements now arranged in the pattern of a period in the periodic table ?

(iii) Name the element which has the (a) largest and (b) smallest atomic number.

(iv) From the above data, explain how the atomic size or atomic radius of the elements change as we go from left to right in a period.

(v) Name one metal, one non-metal and a metalloid out of these elements.

(vi) Why does atomic radius decreases as we move from left to right in a period ?

[CBSE-2012]

Ans. (i)

Li	Be	Be	C	N	O	F
152	111	88	77	74	66	64

(ii) Yes, the elements are now arranged in the pattern of a period of periodic table.

(iii) (a) Li has the smallest atomic number.

(b) F has the largest atomic number.

(iv) Atomic radius decreases on moving from left to right in a period of the periodic table

(v) Metal : Li, Non-metal : C, Metalloid : B

(vi) Force of attraction for the outermost electrons increases because of increase in nuclear charge.

Q.3 (a) State the Modern Periodic Law. How have the elements been arranged in the modem periodic table? Why is it considered that the position of hydrogen in the periodic table is anomalous ?

(b) An element X(2, 8, 2) combines separately with NO_3^- and $(PO_4)^{3-}$ radicals. Write the formulae of the compounds so formed. To which group of the periodic table does the element 'X' belong? Will it form covalent or ionic compounds with these redicals ? How? **[CBSE-2012]**

Ans. (a) Modern Periodic Law Properties of elements (both physical and chemical) are the periodic function of their atomic number.

In increasing order of atomic number because hydrogen can be placed in group 1 with alkali metals as well as with halogens in 17th group.

(b) Three compounds formed :

$X(NO_3)_2$ $X_3(PO_4)_2$

X belongs to 2nd group.

X will form ionic compounds because it is a metal and the radicals are of non-metals.

Q.4 Atoms of seven elements A, B, C, D, E, F and G have a different number of electronic shells but have the same number of electrons in their outermost shells. The elements A and C combine with chlorine to form an acid and common salt respectively. The oxide of element A is liquid at room temperature and is a neutral substance, while the oxides of the remaining six elements are basic in nature. Based on the above information answer the following questions : **[A.I. 2010]**

(i) What could the element A be 7

(ii) Will elements A to G belong to the same period or same group of the periodic table 7

(iii) Write the formula of the compound formed by the reaction of the element A with oxygen.

(iv) Show the formation of the compound by a combination of element C with chlorine with the help of electronic structure.

(v) What would be the ratio of number of combining atoms in a compound formed by the combination of element A with Carbon ?

(vi) Which one of the given elements is likely to have the smallest atomic radius.

Ans. (i) Hydrogen

(ii) Same group

(iii) A_2O/H_2O

(iv) $C\ \curvearrowright\ :\!\ddot{\underset{..}{Cl}}\!: \rightarrow C^+ [:\ddot{\underset{..}{Cl}}\ ]^-$

(v) 4 : 1

(vi) A

CONCEPT APPLICATION LEVEL - III

Q.1 Elements which occupied position in the lother meyer curve, on the peaks, were -
(A) Alkali metals (B) Highly electro positive elements
(C) Elements having large atomic volume (D) All

Q.2 Modern periodic table is based on atomic no. experiments which proved importance of at no. was -
(A) Braggs work on X-ray diffraction
(B) Moseleys work on X-ray spectrum
(C) Mulliken's oil drop experiment
(D) Lother meyer curve plotted between at vol. & at wt.

Q.3 The elements of groups, 1, 2, 13, 14, 15, 16 and 17 are collectively called -
(A) Noble gases (B) Representative or normal elements
(C) Transition elements (D) Inner transition elements

Q.4 The discovery of which of the following group of elements gave a death blow to the Newlands Law -
(A) Inert gases (B) Alkali metals (C) Transuranic element (D) Halogens

Q.5 There are 10 neutrons in the nucleus of the element $_{Z}M^{19}$. It belongs to -
(A) f-block (B) s-block (C) d-block (D) None of these

Q.6 For Rb(Z = 37), points out the number of electrons present in L and N shells respectively -
(A) 8 and 18 (B) 18 and 8 (C) 8 and 8 (D) 2 and 8

Q.7 Z/e ratio for N^{3-}, O^{2-} and F^{-} respectively will be -
(A) 0.7, 0.8 and 0.9 (B) 0.9, 0.8 and 0.7 (C) 7, 8 and 9 (D) 9, 8 and 7

Q.8 The ionic radii of N^{3-}, O^{2-} and F^{-} are respectively given by -
(A) 1.36, 1.40, 1.71 (B) 1.36, 1.71, 1.40
(C) 1.71, 1.40, 1.36 (D) 1.71, 1.36, 1.40

Q.9 Which of the following has largest radius -
(A) $1s^2, 2s^2, 2p^6, 3s^2$ (B) $1s^2, 2s^2, 2p^6, 3s^2, 3p^1$
(C) $1s^2, 2s^2, 2p^6, 3s^2, 3p^3$ (D) $1s^2, 2s^2, 2p^6, 3s^2, 3p^5$

Q.10 The correct order of stability of Al^{+}, Al^{+2}, Al^{+3} is-

(A) $Al^{+3} > Al^{+2} > Al^{+}$
(B) $Al^{+2} > Al^{+3} > Al^{+}$
(C) $Al^{+2} < Al^{+} > Al^{+3}$
(D) $Al^{+3} > Al^{+} > Al^{+2}$

Q.11 Highest ionisation potential in a period is shown by -

(A) Alkali metals
(B) Noble gases
(C) Halogens
(D) Representative elements

Q.12 Electron addition would be easier in -

(A) O (B) O^{+} (C) O^{-} (D) O^{+2}

Q.13 Which of the following process energy is liberated -

(A) $Cl \rightarrow Cl^{+} + e^{-}$ (B) $HCl \rightarrow H^{+} + Cl^{-}$ (C) $Cl + e^{-} \rightarrow Cl^{-}$ (D) $O^{-} + e^{-} \rightarrow O^{-2}$

Q.14 Outermost electronic configuration of the most electronegative element is -

(A) ns^2np^3 (B) ns^2np^6 (C) ns^2 (D) ns^2np^5

Q.15 Which one of the following is incorrect ?

(A) An element which has high electronegativity always has high electron gain enthalpy
(B) Electron gain enthalpy is the property of an isolated atom
(C) Electronegativity is the property of a bonded atom
(D) Both electronegativity and electron gain enthalpy are usually directly related to nuclear charge and inversely related to atomic size

Q.16 $\overset{1}{H C} \equiv \overset{2}{C} - \overset{3}{C}H = \overset{4}{C}H - \overset{5}{C}H_3$ Which carbon atom will show minimum electronegativity -

(A) Fifth (B) Third (C) First (D) Second

Q.17 The ionistion energy of B and Al as compared to Be and Mg are -

(A) Lower (B) Higher (C) Equal (D) None of these

Q.18 Which of the following transitions involve maximum amount of energy -

(A) $M^{-}_{(g)} \rightarrow M_{(g)}$ (B) $M_{(g)} \rightarrow M^{+}_{(g)}$ (C) $M^{+}_{(g)} \rightarrow M^{2+}_{(g)}$ (D) $M^{2+}_{(g)} \rightarrow M^{3+}_{(g)}$

Q.19 The correct values of ionization enthalpies (in kJ mol^{-1}) of Si, P, Cl and S respectively are -

(A) 786, 1012, 999, 1256
(B) 1012, 786, 999, 1256
(C) 786, 1012, 1256, 999
(D) 786, 999, 1012, 1256

Q.20 The correct order of electron affinity of B, C, N, O is -

(A) O > C > N > B
(B) B > N > C > O
(C) O > C > B > N
(D) O > B > C > N

Q.21 Adding electron a neutral gaseous atom usually leads to -

(i) Liberation of energy (ii) Formation of anion

(iii) Proton/electron ratio decrease (iv) Proton/electron ratio increase

Code in -

(A) (i), (iv) (B) (ii), (iii), (iv) (C) (i), (ii), (iv) (D) (i), (ii), (iii)

Q.22 The correct set of decreasing order of electronegativity is -

(A) Li, H, Na (B) Na, H, Li (C) H, Li, Na (D) Li, Na, H

Q.23 Arrange F, C, O, N in the decreasing order of electronegativity -

(A) O > F > N > C (B) F > N > C > O

(C) C > F > N > O (D) F > O > N > C

Q.24 Sodium forms Na^+ ion but it does not form Na^{+2} because -

(A) Very low value of IE_1 and IE_2

(B) Very high value of IE_1 and IE_2

(C) Low value of IE_1 and low value of IE_2

(D) Low value of IE_1 and high value of IE_2

Q.25 Match the following lists and select the correct answer -

	List-I	List-II
(a)	d-block element	i. $1s^2,2s^22s^6,3s^23p^6,4s^1$
(b)	Halogen	ii. $1s^2,2s^22p^6,3s^23p^6$
(c)	Alkali metal	iii. $1s^2,2s^22p^6,3s^23p^63d^6,4s^2$
(d)	Noble gas	iv. $1s^2,2s^22p^5$

Code :

	(a)	(b)	(c)	(d)
(A)	i	ii	iii	iv
(B)	iii	iv	i	ii
(C)	i	iii	ii	iv
(D)	ii	iv	iii	i

Q.26 Which one of the following groups represent a collection of isoelectronic species ?

(At. no. Cs = 55, Br = 35) **[AIEEE-2003]**

(A) N^{3-}, F^-, Na^+ (B) Be, Al^{3+}, Cl^- (C) Ca^{2+}, Cs^+, Br (D) Na^+, Ca^{2+}, Mg^{2+}

Q.27 Which one of the following sets of ions represent the collection of isoelectronic species ?

[AIEEE-2004]

(A) K^+, Cl^-, Mg^{2+}, Sc^{3+} (B) Na^+, Ca^{2+}, Sc^{3+}, F^-

(C) K^+, Ca^{2+}, Sc^{3+}, Cl^- (D) Na^+, Mg^{2+}, Al^{3+}, Cl^-

Q.28 Which one of the following ions has the highest value of ionic radius ? **[AIEEE-2004]**
(A) O^{2-} (B) B^{3+} (C) Li^{+} (D) F^{-}

Q.29 The increasing order of the ionic radii of the given isoelectronic species is- **[AIEEE-2012]**
(A) s^{2-}, Cl^{-}, Ca^{2+}, K^{+} (B) Ca^{2+}, K^{+}, Cl^{-}, S^{2-}
(C) K^{+}, S^{2-}, Ca^{2+}, Cl^{-} (D) Cl^{-}, Ca^{2+}, K^{+}, S^{2-}

Q.30 Which one of the following has largest size ?
(A) Na (B) Na^{+} (C) Na^{-} (D) None of these

Q.31 The decreasing order of the second ionization energy of K, Ca and Ba is
(At. Nos. K = 19, Ca = 20, Ba = 56)
(A) K > Ca > Ba (B) Ca > Ba > K (C) Ba > K > Ca (D) K > Ba > Ca

Q.32 Moving from right to left in a periodic table, the atomic size is- **[IIT-1995]**
(A) Increased (B) Decreased (C) Remains constant (D) None of these

Q.33 The number of paired electrons in oxygen is - **[IIT-1995]**
(A) 6 (B) 16 (C) 8 (D) 32

Q.34 Which of the following has the maximum number of unpaired electrons - **[IIT-1996]**
(A) Mg^{2+} (B) Ti^{3+} (C) V^{3+} (D) Fe^{2+}

Q.35 The correct order of radii is - **[IIT-2000]**
(A) N < Be < B (B) $F^{-} < O^{2-} < N^{3-}$ (C) Na < Li < K (D) $Fe^{3+} < Fe^{2+} < Fe^{4+}$

Direction :

Below Q.No. 36 to Q.No. 37 consist of an 'assertion in column1 and the 'reason' in column 2. Against the specific question number, write in the appropriate space.
(A) If both assertion and reason are **CORRECT**, and reason is the **CORRECT** explanation of the assertion.
(B) If both assertion and reason are **CORRECT**, but reason is not the **CORRECT** explanation of the assertion.
(C) If assertion is **CORRECT** but reason is **INCORRECT**
(D) If assertion is **INCORRECT** reason in **CORRECT**

Q.36 **Assertion :** F atom has a negative electron gain enthalpy than Cl atom. **[IIT-2000]**
Reason : Additional electron are repelled more effectively by 3p electron in Cl atom than by 2p electron in F atom.

Q.37 **Assertion :** LiCl is predominantly a covalent compound. **[IIT-2000]**
Reason : Electronegativity difference between Li and Cl is too small.

Q.38 Element "X" which is solid and having high melting point, form a Chloride "X Cl_3". This element "X" would be in which group of Periodic table **[NTSE-13]**

(A) Na (B) Mg (C) Al (D) Si

Q.39 The first ionisation potential of Na is 5.1 eV. The value of electron gain enthalpy of Na^+ will be- **[JEE Main 2013]**

(A) –10.2 eV (B) + 2.55 eV (C) – 2.55 eV (D) – 5.1 eV

Q.40 False statement for second period elements is **[NTSE-14]**

(A) change in number of electrons produce ions

(B) numbers of protons and electrons are equal in neutral atom

(C) number of neutrons is less than the number of protons in atoms

(D) change in the number of neutrons in atom produces isotopes

Q.41 Neutron less neutral atom is **[NTSE-14]**

(A) H (B) He (C) Na (D) K

Q.42 The last electron of the element of atomic number 31 will have the following quantum numbers **[NTSE-12]**

	n	*l*	m	s
(A)	3	0	0	–1/2
(B)	4	1	–1	–1/2
(C)	3	1	1	+1/2
(D)	4	0	0	+1/2

Q.43 Which one of the following can lose two electrons to attain the configuration of neon ? **[IOS-13]**

(A) Ca (B) C (C) Mg (D) Fe

Q.44 Mercury is the only metal which is liquid at 0°C. This is due to-

(A) very high ionization energy and weak metallic bond

(B) low ionization energy

(C) high atomic weight

(D) high vapour pressure

Q.45 If there were 10 periods in periodic table then maximum number of elements it can have is-

(A) 290 (B) 770 (C) 204 (D) None of these

*****

ANSWER KEY

CONCEPT APPLICATION LEVEL - II

SECTION-A

Q.1	C	Q.2	C	Q.3	B	Q.4	B	Q.5	B	Q.6	D	Q.7	B
Q.8	B	Q.9	C	Q.10	B								

CONCEPT APPLICATION LEVEL - III

Q.1	D	Q.2	B	Q.3	B	Q.4	A	Q.5	D	Q.6	C	Q.7	A
Q.8	C	Q.9	A	Q.10	D	Q.11	B	Q.12	D	Q.13	C	Q.14	D
Q.15	A	Q.16	A	Q.17	A	Q.18	D	Q.19	C	Q.20	C	Q.21	D
Q.22	C	Q.23	D	Q.24	D	Q.25	B	Q.26	A	Q.27	C	Q.28	A
Q.29	B	Q.30	C	Q.31	A	Q.32	A	Q.33	A	Q.34	D	Q.35	B
Q.36	C	Q.37	C	Q.38	C	Q.39	D	Q.40	C	Q.41	A	Q.42	B
Q.43	C	Q.44	A	Q.45	A								

NOTES

NOTES

Printed by Libri Plureos GmbH in Hamburg,
Germany